First edition.

"*Unashamed* is a step-by-step
ing that holy call to stand in
who we are. No apologies. N
the threats—internal and exter
and offers strategies first for su

—LINDA KAY KLEI
Movement That S
How I Broke Free, and founder of Break Free Together

"*Unashamed* is a heartfelt, supportive resource for LGBTQ Christians
finding their place in the church and in the world. I'm so glad Amber
Cantorna created such a vital and important work."

—MIKE McHARGUE, host of *Ask Science Mike*
and author of *Finding God in the Waves*

"Amber Cantorna beautifully radiates God's love and hope for all God's
children as she masterfully weaves together helpful action steps and stories that are both informative and empowering. *Unashamed: A Coming-
Out Guide for LGBTQ Christians* is filled with golden nuggets of hope,
healing, and truth that everyone can benefit from—whether you are
an LGBTQ Christian looking for assistance and encouragement in the
coming-out process, an ally or parent seeking to support a loved one in
the process, or simply someone interested in transforming and growing
in the ever-faithful compassion and love of God. *Unashamed* is a must-
read for everyone!"

—JANE CLEMENTI, cofounder and CEO
of the Tyler Clementi Foundation

"Amber Cantorna has done it again. After the success of her book *Refocusing My Family*, Amber has returned with a practical, readable guide
to the challenges of living authentically. In *Unashamed: A Coming-Out
Guide for LGBTQ Christians*, Amber speaks with the wisdom of someone who has lived through the kind of shame only evangelicalism can
impart. For those with the courage to let the world know who they
are, *Unashamed* will guide you, lovingly and competently, one step at
a time."

—PAULA STONE WILLIAMS, Pastor,
TED speaker, LGBTQ advocate

"As the mother of a gay son, I wish my child would have had *Unashamed* when he came out. With practicality, compassion, and wisdom that comes from personal experience, Amber Cantorna broaches coming out in a way that no other book has done. As both a mother and the leader of Free Mom Hugs, I will most definitely recommend this book to all LGBTQ Christians who are on the journey of embracing their deepest, truest selves."

—SARA CUNNINGHAM, founder of Free Mom Hugs and author of *How We Sleep at Night: A Mother's Memoir*

"As the gay, closeted son of a Southern Baptist pastor, I didn't think I'd ever come out. It was too scary. But in my late 20s, I began to plan my coming-out process. I was paralyzed with fear. I had no guidance, no resources, and very little confidence. I felt like the only person in the world who'd gone through this. Thanks to Amber Cantorna's book *Unashamed*, no closeted, Christian, LGBTQ person should ever have to feel that way again. This book clearly and practically lays out a set of best practices for people who want to come out but aren't sure how. Coming out is never easy, but, thanks to Amber, it just got a whole lot easier."

—B. T. HARMAN, creator of the blog and podcast *Blue Babies Pink*

"This is Amber Cantorna at her best! She takes the nitty-gritty experiences that every LGBTQ person of faith experiences and breaks them down in an incredibly accessible way. Everyone who reads this book will leave with a greater understanding of what it is to be queer and a deeper understanding of steps to take that will lead toward wholeness in accepting God's love for all. Reading it feels like having a personal coach on all things LGBTQ and Christian. It's just so good!"

—CANDICE CZUBERNAT, founder and therapist at the Christian Closet

"I wish I could go back and give this book to fifteen-year-old me. Amber has expertly consolidated advice born from people who have previously walked this road of faith and coming out. If you find this book in your hands, consider yourself lucky. May it enlighten you on your path."

—MATTHIAS ROBERTS, psychotherapist and host of *Queerology: A Podcast on Belief and Being*

"*Unashamed: A Coming-Out Guide for LGBTQ Christians* is bound to be an enduring addition to the resource shelf for LGBTQ Christians and others seeking to support them. Speaking with the authority of someone who has persevered through her own difficult coming out, Amber Cantorna puts into words the lessons many of us have had to learn through hard-fought trial and error. What's most compelling about the book is the breadth of wisdom it offers on the coming-out process, from the practical (such as considering one's safety and self-sufficiency before coming out) to the emotional (such as tending to one's own grieving heart in the face of rejection). This book is full of candid advice that is relevant to anyone navigating the challenging season of coming out."

—DAVID and CONSTANTINO KHALAF, authors of
Modern Kinship: A Queer Guide to Christian Marriage

"Every new journey can be terrifying, none more so than the path to a more authentic version of ourselves. In *Unashamed*, Amber Cantorna provides a clear, encouraging, and life-giving travel companion for LGBTQ Christians—and the people who love them—walking into the wide-open spaces of their truest selves. It will be an invaluable tool for those navigating the personal and relational challenges of coming out, and essential reading for allies hoping to walk alongside well."

—JOHN PAVLOVITZ, author of *A Bigger Table*
and *Hope and Other Superpowers*

"Amber Cantorna's *Unashamed* is a rich yet intensely practical resource for every LGBT+ person who is wrestling to step out of the closet within a Christian context. For so many LGBT+ Christians, there is a profound sense of loneliness and disorientation as we seek to navigate coming out and reconciling our faith and sexuality. This book boldly shines the light of truth and love, helping to guide the reader on a path away from shame and toward wholeness as they embrace their God-given queer identity. I will be recommending this book to the many brave LGBT+ Christians I know who are embarking on this journey of liberation."

—BRANDAN ROBERTSON, Lead Pastor, Missiongathering
Christian Church in San Diego and author of
True Inclusion: Creating Communities of Radical Embrace

"Amber Cantorna speaks with the voice of experience—her own and those who have reached out to her for guidance. Amber provides tools for members of the LGBTQ community and those who love them to come out, set boundaries, and flourish as wonderfully created children of God. As a member of clergy and a psychotherapist, I will recommend this book to my congregants and clients who need to know they are loved by God just as they are."

—**NICOLE M. GARCIA**, Director of Congregational Care, Mount Calvary Lutheran Church in Boulder, Colorado, and a licensed professional counselor with the Umbrella Collective

"*Unashamed* is an insightful guide particularly intended for evangelical Christians whose gay or transgender identity has led to broken relationships. Amber Cantorna's personal experience provides practical suggestions for those navigating the rocky road of coming out. She provides hope for those who have experienced rejection from both church and family while recognizing that families with LGBTQ members all have a coming-out process. Best of all is the truth that unconditional love is possible."

—**JEAN HODGES**, PFLAG National President Emerata

"Narratives like this are sorely needed to fill the void that LGBTQ people of faith often experience as we navigate our families, friends, and those who say they love us but not our LGBTQ identity. Cantorna uses her personal experience to help those who are seeking to reconcile their faith with their sexual orientation or gender identity. She fosters family relationships and open dialogue with others in their faith communities. It is a very welcome resource and will prove helpful to many."

—**LISBETH M. MELÉNDEZ RIVERA**, Director of Faith Outreach and Training, Human Rights Campaign

Unashamed

A Coming-Out Guide for LGBTQ Christians

AMBER CANTORNA

WESTMINSTER
JOHN KNOX PRESS
LOUISVILLE · KENTUCKY

First edition
Published by Westminster John Knox Press
Louisville, Kentucky

19 20 21 22 23 24 25 26 27 28—10 9 8 7 6 5 4 3 2 1

Book design by Drew Stevens
Cover design by Barbara LeVan Fisher, www.levanfisherdesign.com

Library of Congress Cataloging-in-Publication Data

Names: Cantorna, Amber, author.
Title: Unashamed : a coming-out guide for LGBTQ Christians / Amber Cantorna.
Description: First edition. | Louisville, Kentucky : Westminster John Knox
  Press, 2018. | Includes bibliographical references. |
  Identifiers: LCCN 2018044505 (print) | LCCN 2019007020 (ebook) | ISBN
  9781611649376 (ebk.) | ISBN 9780664265052 (pbk. : alk. paper)
Subjects: LCSH: Gays—Religious life. | Sexual minorities—Religious life. |
  Homosexuality—Religious aspects—Christianity.
Classification: LCC BV4596.G38 (ebook) | LCC BV4596.G38 C36 2019 (print) |
  DDC 277.3/08308664—dc23
LC record available at https://lccn.loc.gov/2018044505

To every LGBTQ person who has wrestled in isolation,
who has felt the sting of rejection,
who has been scarred by religion,
or who has lost family in the name of love;
to those who have found the courage
to live transparently
in the eyes of others
and to those who do not yet feel safe enough
to make their identity known—
this book is for you.

You are seen, you are heard,
you are loved,
and you are enough.

Contents

Introduction   vii

1. **You Are Not Broken**   1
   Demolishing Internalized Homophobia/Transphobia

2. **Claiming Hope**   19
   *Reestablishing Your Worth as a Child of God
   and Fostering Self-Acceptance*

3. **We Need One Another**   33
   Building an Affirming Community

4. **How Do I Know If I'm Ready?**   49
   Preparing to Come Out

5. **Taking the Leap of Faith**   65
   Coming Out to Your Loved Ones

6. **Boundaries Are Not Disrespectful**   85
   Setting Healthy Boundaries

7. **Am I Worth It?**   103
   The Value of Tending to Your Soul

8. **"I Love You, but . . ."**   117
   Coping with Conditional Love

9. **If Your Heart Is Aching**   133
   Restoring What's Been Lost

10. **Did You Not Know What the Divine Can Do
    with Your Diversity?**   151
    Embracing Who You Are

Acknowledgments   155
Notes   157
Recommended Resources   159

Introduction

It was a snowy Saturday afternoon in Denver, Colorado, when I showed up to lead a workshop at the 2018 Q Christian Fellowship Conference. Together with Susan Cottrell of FreedHearts, we led a sixty-minute session on "Navigating Life and Relationships with Non-Affirming Families." Anticipating the need for a presentation on this topic, the conference team arranged for us to have the largest workshop room available. Just as they expected, when the doors opened, hundreds of people (in fact, one-third of the conference attendees) made their way in and packed out the room. This was my first indication that the topic of coming out to conservative families was tremendously underrepresented in the LGBTQ Christian community.

Susan and I planned to divide our hour of time into two parts. The first half hour would be spent discussing tools and tips for coming out, and the second half hour we would open it up for Q&A. We wanted to allow plenty of time to engage with the audience and address their concerns. But we were *not* prepared for the overwhelming need we were about to confront. As soon as we opened the floor for questions, a sea of hands immediately shot into the air. There was an audible gasp of shock and surprise that suctioned the oxygen from the room. I was stunned and a bit alarmed that the petition for questions was so vast. There was an obvious desire and need for these people to be heard.

For months, I'd received a steady stream of emails and Facebook messages from people seeking advice or wanting to share their story with me. It numbered in the hundreds. So yes, I knew there was a need to address this topic. But to witness it in such a tangible way and visibly see the lives that are being affected by rejection and pain in such startling numbers made one thing very apparent: LGBTQ Christians are desperate for guidance on how to navigate the unexpected journey of coming out. They've been backed into a corner by religion, taught to be ashamed of who they are, and lived in fear of being abandoned by both God and those they love if the truth about their identity leaks out. They want to live authentically, but they lack the needed resources to guide them. The books available to us thus far are limited to theological reconciliation. But the questions that arise about how to practically live out abound.

There was no way that Susan and I could begin to address all the questions people had in the room of our workshop that day. We picked a random hand out of the myriad of those raised and answered as many questions as we possibly could in that thirty-minute time frame. But we barely scratched the surface of the stories and questions represented. Following the session, we both stayed, offering to talk with anyone who still had a burning question they wanted to ask. Each person carried a story, a struggle they were up against in the face of coming out, and a desire to be seen. I wanted to stay all night and talk to each of them; I wanted to validate their journeys, stories, and struggles; I wanted them to know they weren't alone; and more than anything, I wanted them to know that they had nothing to be ashamed of—that they could embrace and love the person that they are, because who they are is beautiful and reflects the very image of God. As the line wound down and the last person left for the night, I couldn't help but think about how many people didn't stay but still had unanswered questions lingering in their hearts. Recognizing the magnitude of the need that day was what birthed the book you're now holding.

At first, I didn't know if I was ready to write another book. Writing my first book (a memoir of my own coming-out journey) had taken an emotional toll on me, I was just winding down from a national book tour, and I had a few other projects I was hoping to accomplish before returning to writing. But I couldn't ignore the request from so many people seeking guidance, nor the wind of God's spirit speaking to my soul that this book needed to be written—now.

So this book is my labor of love to each of you who identify as an LGBTQ person of faith. It is written to those of you who have lost your faith, to those of you who are desperately trying to hold onto your faith, and to those of you who want to reclaim your faith.

It is written for each of you who have emailed or messaged me on social media and shared your coming-out story and the pain you have faced as a result. It is written for the preacher's kid, the missionary kid, the church kid, the homeschooled kid, the "Adventures in Odyssey" kid, the bullied kid, and the kid who never quite knew how to fit in.

It is written for the outcast, the leper, the black sheep, and those of you who feel like you are somehow never quite enough.

It is written for the LGBTQ person who did everything you could to be the "perfect Christian," who tried to pattern your life after the Focus on the Family model, who went through ex-gay therapy, conversion therapy, and psychological abuse, suppressing your sexual feelings and desires because you were told you had to conform to the literal interpretation of Scripture in order to be acceptable to God. It is written for those of you who were forced into celibacy or a marriage to a person of the opposite sex because someone convinced you that God required it of you.

It is written for those of you who are thinking about coming out, for those who are in the process of coming out, for those who have already come out, and for those who have previously come out but who ended up back in the closet again due to fear.

This book is for those of you who struggle with worthiness, who were told that setting boundaries was disrespectful, who believed the lie that God despises who you are, who carry suffocating shame about your identity, who feel terrified to be seen, and who feel so isolated in your struggle that you don't know if you can live another day. This book is for *you*.

I want you to know that I see you. I see who you are. I see

the struggles you face every day, the fear that overwhelms you, the pain that is so heavy it takes effort just to keep breathing. I see *you*.

You are not alone.

This book will not give you all the answers. To attempt that is an impossible and unrealistic task. Each of your stories is unique and accompanied with its own set of challenges. But what I hope to provide you in these pages are guideposts that will equip you to successfully navigate the journey ahead. As you walk through the forests, the mountains, and the valleys of coming out, may these words be markers that light your way and provide you with the confidence and strength you need to not only endure but to thrive.

I am not a licensed therapist, nor do I claim to be. The information in this book is based on my years of experience, research, and study as an LGBTQ Christian advocate and leader, and is formed out of the hundreds of conversations I've had with people who have reached out to me for guidance and support. This book is not meant to be a replacement for therapy, but rather a tool to help guide you along your path to healing and wholeness. You will benefit most from this book by reading it in order. It is designed to take a holistic approach to coming out and builds upon each concept as it progresses. While jumping ahead to the part that currently applies to you the most can be tempting, I encourage you to start at the beginning in order to learn the most about yourself and gain the most out of each idea as it extends the one preceding it.

Know that you do not walk alone, though at times it may feel lonely. Countless others out there are also trying to navigate this same path. Some of them you will meet in the pages of this book;* others you will meet along the way. Writing this book is also my way of journeying with each of you and doing what I can to give you a compass for your trail. My hope is that as you go through this book, you will discover another set of

---

*All the stories in this book represent actual people. The names of some have been changed for the sake of privacy.

footprints as well and realize that God is also walking alongside you, and always has been.

Have courage, my friend. Don't let fear win. Come, let's journey together and learn what it means to live unashamed.

NOTE TO PARENTS AND ALLIES

At the end of each chapter you will find a section specifically written to parents and allies that suggests practical ways to come alongside your LGBTQ loved one and support them in their journey. I hope you will find these notes useful as you continue to learn and grow in your own experience of what it means to live and love like Jesus.

1

You Are Not Broken

Demolishing Internalized Homophobia/Transphobia

Never let fear determine who you are, and never let where you have been determine where you are going.
—Constantine "Cus" D'Amato

By the age of eight, Isaac knew that he was different from his older brother. He couldn't quite pinpoint why, but he knew he didn't fit the mold. Within the next couple years, Isaac had figured out that whatever made him different also made him unacceptable to the culture in which he lived. With parents who were deeply invested in a church plant and who served in leadership roles at all three services each weekend, there was a standard in place of what was expected of godly, Christian children. Isaac didn't measure up. According to his family, his church, and his faith, being gay was not only detestable, it was offensive and repugnant. Ashamed, Isaac tried to hide and repress this part of his identity for years—first by dating girls, then through regular fasting and prayer, and eventually by flat-out lying about his sexual orientation when people asked, just so that he could blend in. Isaac refused to admit his feelings for men to anyone—even to himself.

But the mix of curiosity, testosterone, and puberty caught up to Isaac in high school, and the friendship he had with the pastor's son turned sexual. That friend then used Isaac as a scapegoat when confronted by his parents, which landed Isaac in front of an emergency staff meeting at their church.

With his parents in attendance and in front of all of the staff, Isaac was outed, dehumanized, and humiliated. Grappling for a way to be redeemed and restored to a place of belonging, Isaac retreated even further into the closet and suppressed all emotion that revealed his true sexual orientation. In the coming years, Isaac enrolled in ex-gay therapy, got involved in an intensive prayer and discipleship internship to cleanse his soul, and married a woman in an attempt to reconcile with his family and his friends, and with God.

When Erin O. White was twenty-two, she simultaneously fell in love with Catholicism and with a woman. In her book, *Given Up for You,*[1] Erin talks about her desire for both romantic and divine love and her wrestling between these two worlds. Erin longed to connect to God, but she also longed to connect with human flesh. Feeling unable to reconcile the division inside her, she decided to divulge a small piece of her heart to her therapist, hoping for helpful tools that would reconcile these two worlds. But instead, she was told that she would be a more complete human being if she was in a heterosexual relationship and that if she continued in her current relationship with her girlfriend, there was nothing for the two of them to accomplish together in therapy. Devastated and betrayed by the one person she trusted, Erin left her counseling session that day never to return. The words from her therapist and the message behind them permeated her soul for years, causing doubt, fear, shame, and brokenness. Knowing she couldn't have both God and her girlfriend, she let go of one of the two things most precious to her for the sake of the other.

Paul knew he was transgender* by the time he was three or four years old. He didn't hate being a boy. He just knew he

*When wondering the difference between sexuality (being gay, lesbian, or straight) and gender identity (being cisgender or transgender), it is often described in these terms: your sexuality is who you want to go to bed *with*, your gender identity is who you want to go to bed *as*. Going to bed *with* a person of the same sex or a person of the opposite sex determines your sexuality, and going to bed *as* a male or female determines your gender identity. There are also those who are bisexual (attracted to men and women), as well as those who are gender nonconforming, gender fluid, or gender non-binary (meaning they don't fit into either male or female categories, or prefer not to be labeled as such.)

wasn't one. With the innocence that comes in childhood, Paul naively thought that when he got to the age of attending kindergarten, a gender fairy would arrive and allow him to choose which gender he wanted to be. But because that gender fairy never appeared, Paul never got to tell the fairy what he really wanted—which was to be a girl. So consequently, Paul just continued to live his life. He went to college, got married, and had kids. He climbed the ladder of success, becoming the CEO of a large religious nonprofit, the host of a national television show, and a preaching pastor at several megachurches across America. But the further along in life Paul went, the less he was able to deny the call from God to be authentic. When that day of authenticity came and Paul transitioned to Paula, she in turn lost every one of the prestigious positions she'd previously held. She went from a well-educated, highly esteemed church leader to a demoted individual seen as shameful, embarrassing, and deceived. In the span of a day, everything for Paula changed.

Unfortunately, all three of these friends of mine have stories steeped in homophobia.* For Isaac, the homophobia of his parents and church leadership caused him to suppress his true identity and hide his real self. For Erin, her therapist's homophobia led Erin to believe that she could not be a vessel of love for both her girlfriend and for God. And for Paula, the transphobia of those she worked with cost her every one of the esteemed positions she had worked so hard to obtain. If you are holding this book in your hands and you identify as part of the LGBTQ community, I can say with 100 percent certainty that you have experienced homophobia in some form or another. It may be in the form of comments your parents have made about gay marriage, or the derogatory jokes your classmates laughed at in school. Perhaps your job doesn't value or

---

*For the purposes of this book, I use the term "homophobia" to refer to the unreasonable fear people have toward the LGBTQ population as a whole. This includes transgender people. While I recognize that transphobia and homophobia are distinct, I use "homophobia" as an umbrella term throughout this book.

recognize the need of having a nondiscrimination clause that includes sexual orientation and gender identity among those protected. Maybe you even work for a Christian organization or church that would instantly fire you if you came out. These are just a few of many examples that can cause us to feel unsafe and unprotected in our own skin. Sadly, in our current society, it is impossible for any LGBTQ person to completely escape homophobia. It permeates our culture, our church pews, our political party lines, our work policies, and our daily lives.

If we are going to learn how to embrace ourselves and love ourselves into healing and wholeness, we must dismantle the homophobia that resides within our own hearts. To do that, we need to start by naming and defining the thing that has caused some of our deepest pain. For the purposes of this book, I have created a working definition for the terms *homophobia* and *internalized homophobia* so that we have a common understanding and a baseline from which to start:

> **Homophobia:** An unreasonable fear held by straight, cisgender* people toward the LGBTQ community.
> **Internalized homophobia:** The innate belief that your sexual orientation or gender identity makes you undeserving of an equal place in society—that you are not enough and are instead rendered unlovable by others and unacceptable in the eyes of God.

As we move through this chapter, we dissect the layers of obvious and subtle homophobia that we experience in our society and learn how that perspective is internalized when we fail to recognize it. We also discuss the role of shame and fear, how our view of God determines the level of our own self-acceptance, and what it means to foster that self-acceptance in our deepest parts. I know this topic may feel a little daunting or intimidating, but until we can name, understand, and dismantle the fear that holds us captive, we cannot move forward into an unashamed life.

*Cisgender: A person whose gender identity corresponds with the biological sex assigned to them at birth.

LAYERS OF OBVIOUS AND
SUBTLE HOMOPHOBIA

There are differing degrees and layers in which we experience homophobia when moving through the world. Some are blatant and obvious—like when you're holding your boyfriend's hand as you walk down the street and someone calls you a "faggot," or when you announce on Facebook that you just got engaged to your girlfriend and someone feels it is within their right to inform you that you're destined for hell. Those are deliberate ways that, usually through some kind of verbal sneer, people communicate to you that who you are is unacceptable. These experiences hurt and are embarrassing, often because they are done in front of the eyes and ears of others.

But the number of times that we experience obvious, external homophobia is drastically small compared to the number of times that we experience the subtle homophobia that creeps into our everyday lives. Sometimes it is presented in such a faint and clever way that we fail to even recognize it for what it is. A few examples of subtle homophobia would be:

—When your parent introduces your significant other as a "friend" to people at a holiday gathering

—When your pastor says that everyone is welcome, but then keeps coming up with excuses as to why you can't help in the nursery or lead a Sunday school class

—When your employer says the company supports you as a transperson, but does nothing to make sure gender-neutral bathrooms are available for you

—When your friend says that they accept the fact that you're bisexual, but then only shows enthusiasm when you talk about dating a person of the opposite sex

—When you come out to someone you love and they say that it changes nothing, but then they slowly distance from you more and more until the bond you previously shared no longer exists

Subtle homophobia presents itself in endless ways. But regardless of how it manifests, the root of homophobia is fear: Fear of what other people will think. Fear of losing their reputation. Fear of endangering their soul. Fear of the unknown. *Fear.* And fear of what people don't know or don't understand, when left unconfronted, keeps them captive to a world in which they must remain comfortable to survive. We can't change the way that other people respond to us, but we can change whether or not we absorb their fear and internalize it as our own.

HOW DOES HOMOPHOBIA BECOME INTERNALIZED?

After my friend Isaac was outed to his parents and church leadership, the degree of homophobia he experienced from them sent him into a tailspin. Rebelling against the God he'd been taught would send him to hell for being gay, he engaged in every chance to be destructive to both his body and his soul. He drank, he partied, he slept around, he inflicted physical wounds on himself—all in attempt to numb the pain and ignore the hurt that was brewing beneath the surface. Unhappy and unable to find fulfillment, Isaac felt empty inside. Eventually, the light at the end of the tunnel disappeared, and Isaac knocked on death's door one night by attempting suicide.

For Erin, she took her therapist's disapproval as gospel truth rather than recognizing it for the homophobia that it was. Because of that, she internalized the belief that she could not love both the Catholic Church and her girlfriend. That division caused years of striving to fit the heteronormative culture and blend in with the straight world. When it came to planning her wedding, Erin took on the role of the feminine bride and wanted everything to be just the way it would have been if she were straight. She wanted the dress, the ceremony, the symbolic words that marked the day like "wedding," "marriage," and "wife." In essence, she wanted all the things she'd always dreamed of growing up and didn't want to be seen as different just because the person she was marrying was a female.

In 2003, when Massachusetts was the first state to legalize gay marriage, Erin struggled to celebrate the victory in the same way that her wife did. Despising the fact that the government held the power to determine whether her marriage was "real" or not, Erin didn't want the union she'd shared with her wife up to that point to be seen as a sham. If it was only now legal to enter into gay marriage, then what was it that she and her wife had been sharing since their wedding day? Erin detested the fact that she wasn't equal in the eyes of the government and that she had to fight for rights that would be freely given to her if she were straight. When it came time to talk about children, Erin was envious that it was so easy for her friends to conceive and embarrassed and ashamed that she couldn't conceive the same way. Frustrated and distanced from the God she once loved so dearly, she wrestled with her desires to blend in with the straight world.

After coming out as transgender, Paula had a difficult road ahead of her, not just because of her transition, but because of what that transition meant to the evangelical world in which she'd lived. Facing the anger of her church members and friends, as well as many complete strangers, they all felt they had the right to tell her how God felt about her gender dysphoria. Many saw Paul as their only gentle male role model and looked to him as their rock and touchstone. But (unless you are transgender yourself), it is impossible for any of us to know what it feels like to be in a wrongly gendered body, just as it is equally impossible for straight people to know what it is like to be gay, lesbian, or bisexual. With statistics from the Trevor Project stating that 40 percent of transgender people attempt suicide, they are among the most at-risk populations in our society.[2]

For everyone in Paula's life who felt the need to part ways, she decided to simply give them a pass. She agreed to not contact them and asked them not to contact her. She began again, starting over by creating a new life for herself. Setting boundaries to keep herself safe and healthy, Paula did what she had to in order to move on and tried her hardest not to internalize the ugly comments and hateful words being spewed at her in the name of God.

The most damaging part about homophobia and transphobia is that when we hear someone else's opinion of us and don't intentionally take steps to reject it and deny its truth, we inadvertently (and often subconsciously) accept it as fact by default. It internalizes within us, becoming part of our own beliefs about our mind, body, and soul. Whether beliefs about ourselves or the culture in which we live, it is easy to embody other people's opinions if we have not examined and formed our own. I may hear someone comment that gun violence isn't a problem in the United States, and if I lived under a rock (or in a Bible bubble like I did for the first twenty years of my life), I may think that person is right. My ignorance may lead me to accept this person's opinion as fact rather than researching it for myself. But a simple Internet search will tell you that, in truth, over twenty-six thousand children and teens have died due to gun violence since the Columbine shooting took place in 1999.[3] Clearly this problem needs to be addressed.

The same goes for homophobia. Without a moral foundation to ground us in the knowledge that we are valued human beings who deserve an equal place in society, it is easy to internalize other people's fears as our own. Fear will tell us that we're the only one who is crazy enough to show up gay, bi, or trans in a conservative Christian family. Fear will tell us it is impossible to love both God and our bodies. Fear will tell us that our gender identity or sexual orientation excludes us from a loving place in both our biological family and in the family of God. Fear can convince us of just about anything—*but that doesn't mean fear is right.*

When we are born, the first people group we look to in order to try and find ourselves reflected is our immediate family. Usually (unless you are adopted) you find yourself reflected in the physical features of your parents—their skin color, their height, perhaps you have your dad's nose or your mom's smile. Finding ourselves reflected in our immediate family provides a sense of belonging. You have your tribe, and you know that because you can see your physical and personality traits reflected in one another. But if we look at our immediate family and do not see ourselves reflected, as is often the case with adopted children, we feel disconnected and a seed of shame is planted inside our hearts about what makes us different.

Though there is believed to be a genetic component to being LGBTQ in some cases, most people do not see that reflected in their immediate family. If they do find it reflected, it is most often in a relative, such as an uncle who is gay or a gender non-binary cousin they discover later on in life. It is rare that LGBTQ children will see themselves reflected in their immediate family from their elementary years. Therefore, at that pivotal point in childhood when kids are the most curious and most looking for belonging, it is easy for an LGBTQ child or youth to feel isolated when they realize that their parents and siblings are all different from them (i.e., straight, cisgender people). Feeling lonely in their primary tribe and without a place to express their authentic self from a young age, those seeds of shame begin to grow. In time, not seeing themselves reflected in their family or society, combined with the sly and subtle ways people around them express homophobia, makes it easy for that child to internalize those fears and question their place in the world as they grow older and discover more of who they are.

This is compounded even further when we look at our faith communities and don't see ourselves reflected. Unlike racial minorities who have the ability to find a church of their own ethnicity, LGBTQ people have to fight extremely hard for their place at the table of God's family. To be welcomed in the church pews isn't enough. We need a place to belong. So if you are unable to engage in an affirming church community, and you don't see yourself embraced and reflected in the church you currently attend, those undercurrents of not belonging continue to water and grow those seeds of shame.

Note, too, that LGBTQ people can often hide their sexual orientation or gender identity. It isn't always as obvious as other identities, such as the color of your skin. And when we are able to hide it, we can become bound to secrecy, which in turn also fosters shame. To begin piecing this together, we need to understand the difference between guilt and shame, and the contributing role that shame plays in our own internalized homophobia.

THE ROLE OF SHAME

Brené Brown, storyteller and research professor at the University of Houston, is known worldwide for her research on shame, courage, and vulnerability. She's perhaps one of my greatest heroes because she confronts these often taboo topics in a way that is so countercultural but that could heal our world if we would embrace it. I can't talk about shame without referencing her work, both because of its brilliance and its groundbreaking power to move and shape our culture.

For those in the LGBTQ community, it almost goes without saying, but for the straight people reading this book, you need to know that shame plays a significant role in the lives of LGBTQ people. Shame is something that can hold you captive, convince you that you're not worth fighting for, and at its strongest point, even take lives. It is something we have to face in order to be free. To do that, we first have to understand the difference between guilt and shame.

The simplest way to break it down is that guilt says, "I've *done* something wrong," whereas shame says, "I *am* something wrong." Guilt is when I know I've eaten more calories than my diet allows and I have to weigh in tomorrow. Shame is the belief that I am ugly and disgusting because of my weight and nobody is going to love me. Guilt is the knowledge that you lied when your best friend asked you if you were gay. Shame is the internalized belief that because you're gay (or bi or trans), you're unworthy of love or belonging. Brown says that shame is a focus on self, whereas guilt is a focus on behavior.

So how do we resolve shame over our LGBTQ identity? We have to name it. In her TED Talk "Listening to Shame," Brené Brown says, "If you put shame in a Petri dish, it needs three things to grow exponentially: secrecy, silence, and judgment. If you put the same amount of shame in a Petri dish and douse it with empathy, it can't survive. The two most powerful words when we're in struggle are 'me too.'"[4] We have to identify and name our shame. We have to walk out of secrecy and into vulnerability. We have to speak out about those things that have kept us silenced. And we have to walk away from the judgment of others and into the empathetic arms of those who will embrace us for all that we are.

Very much like shame, we also have to be able to identify and name homophobia. Unfortunately, homophobia is something that we will continue to encounter our entire lives. Even with the Supreme Court ruling that granted marriage equality in 2015, I don't think any of us will outlive the reality of homophobia in our culture. And transgender people have even further to go to reach equality and safety in our society. But if we can identify homophobia and transphobia for the horrible, dehumanizing behavior that it is and name it as such, it will have no place to internalize in our hearts or manifest in our lives. Just like shame, homophobia and transphobia cannot live inside of us if we bring it to the light. We must recognize it, name it, and refuse to allow it to inhabit our hearts. We must also be able to pinpoint our fears and know which fears are valid and which fears need to be obliterated completely.

REAL FEAR VS. FALSE FEAR

Something we often forget (but is a great tool on this journey toward living unashamed) is that there is real fear and there is false fear. If you have a fear of the dentist, that (in my opinion) is a very legitimate fear. I know from multiple experiences that there is a good chance that a trip to the dentist is going to cause you some pain.

Other fears are not so valid. A couple of years ago I was in Las Vegas and had the chance to go to the top of Paris Las Vegas's half-size replica of the Eiffel Tower. Entering the elevator and beginning the ascent to the 460-foot-high viewing area above, a fear of heights washed over me for the first time in my life. I watched the world beneath me get smaller and my anxiety started to mount. This fear was not something I'd ever experienced in my childhood, teens, or twenties. In fact, I'd been to the top of the real Eiffel Tower in Paris when I was a teenager without giving its height a second thought. I've been to many high places and always enjoyed the view. But with the arrival of my thirties, something in my equilibrium was changing and I suddenly felt very afraid. I tried to be tough and pretend like I wasn't afraid. I was even upset with myself for feeling scared because I had never before experienced a fear of heights. I wanted to force myself to face my fear and overcome it. But on the elevator ride back down to solid ground, I looked at my wife with wide eyes and said, "I have definitely developed a fear of heights!" I'm pretty sure she laughed at me.

When we evaluate the more serious fears in our lives, we find that, just like the smaller ones, some are more valid than others. The trick is separating the fears that are real and can manifest in our lives in big ways from those that seem big but, when confronted, hold no actual weight.

The reality is that being LGBTQ does come with some real and valid fears: fear of losing your job, fear of being rejected by your family, fear for your safety, fear of being forced out of church leadership or abandoned by friends you thought were reliable. Those are real fears that unfortunately do play a significant role in your coming-out process.

But I want you to see that the thing perhaps you fear the most is actually a falsehood and is built on lies that hold absolutely no weight at all.

IS BEING GAY A SIN IN THE EYES OF GOD?
REDISCOVERING OUR PLACE
IN GOD'S NARRATIVE

If just reading the title of this section causes you significant anxiety, I invite you to close your eyes and take several slow, deep breaths. I recognize that it's possible that many people have told you, yes, embracing your LGBTQ identity is a sin. Fear may intensify in your belly because you've believed it to be true. So take a minute, fill your lungs with air, hold it to the count of three, and then slowly exhale through your nose.

Once you've done that, I want you to read these words through a fresh lens—a lens of full acceptance—by putting your name in the blank and giving your heart permission to hear what it so desperately longs to hear:

> But now, O _____, listen to the LORD who created you.
> O _____, the one who formed you says,
> "*Do not be afraid*, for I have ransomed you.
> I have called you by name. You are mine."
> (Isa. 43:1, emphasis added)

Let the truth of those words sink deep into your soul. Repeat them again if needed. When you're ready, continue and let your heart hear these next words of truth:

> Do not be afraid, for I am with you.
> Do not be discouraged, for I am *your* God.
> I will strengthen you and help you.
> I will hold you up with my victorious right hand.
> (Isa. 41:10, emphasis added)

And finally . . .

> There is no fear in love; but perfect love casts out fear, because fear involves torment. But he who fears has not been made perfect in love.
> (1 John 4:18 NKJV)

If you're thinking to yourself, *But that verse is for other people, it doesn't apply to me. Being LGBTQ disqualifies me from God's love and protection*, listen to me closely when I say that *you are wrong*. The fear we hold that God despises us because of our sexual orientation or gender identity is a myth that you have been brainwashed to believe. It simply is not so. The good news of God's love is for *you*, and it is time to rediscover your place in God's narrative.

It is impossible for me to unpack the clobber passages here in a way that will help you reconcile your faith with your sexuality.* That is an entire book in itself. We are very fortunate to now have a handful of excellent books written by biblical scholars who have done that much-needed work for us and laid it out in a very comprehensive and understandable way. If that is something you haven't done yet, I highly recommend you look at the Resources section in the back for a list of books I recommend on helping you understand what the Bible really says on the topic of same-sex relationships. But for the purposes of this chapter on homophobia, I am suggesting that we change the lens we've used to view God in the past and give God's love a fresh new look. Look with a lens that holds no shame. I believe that, in doing so, we will realize that there is actually nothing to be afraid of—that we hold full access to the love of God and have the same equality in the eyes of God as every other human being on this planet.

Part of the challenge we face as Christians is that we've been taught to not trust our feelings. We've suppressed that inner voice that speaks to our spirit, dismissed it, and labeled it as "our sinful nature," when in reality we are actually suppressing the voice of God. We are diminishing the very vessel that God uses to speak to our souls—the Holy Spirit. We've come to trust the conservative church more than we trust that inner voice. Let me tell you that as a beloved child of God, you don't need pastors or church leaders to hear from God on your behalf. You have full access to hear from God yourself.

---

*The clobber passages are the texts in the Bible that non-affirming Christians commonly reference as claims against same-sex relationships.

Pay attention and listen to that still, small voice. Give yourself permission to trust it. Yes, glean wisdom from people ahead of you in the journey and read information from trusted biblical scholars, but listen to the instrument by which God imparts his love into your soul.

For Isaac, his breakthrough came when he finally started listening to that small, inner voice for himself. When he did, he heard for the first time that being gay was not something he needed to change; it was actually something beautiful to be embraced and affirmed. Isaac began to let God out of the box he'd created for God to live in and rediscover the narrative of love. He realized that the way he understood God had to change. Isaac had hated himself for years because he believed that God hated him. Once his view of God began to shift, he began to see himself through the lens of love—the lens that said God created him to be gay and there was no reason for shame.

Isaac is now on staff at an affirming church, helping other people readjust their view of God, affirming their place in God's family, and advocating for the oppressed and marginalized. He's thrilled to finally be dating the man of his dreams and is continuing to heal from the pain of his past. While that doesn't mean that everything is perfect, Isaac's heart is finally free to breathe and to be who he was meant to be all along.

In Erin's case, she struggled for years to find her place in the Catholic Church as a lesbian believer. In fact, for a long time she didn't attend mass at all. The words of her therapist continued to haunt her and make her feel unworthy. It wasn't until she went to meet a priest in search of affirmation and belonging that she finally had an epiphany. That day she realized that she didn't need to hear someone else's approval of her, or someone else's opinion of what God thought of her relationship. She needed to hear this from God for herself. In search of acceptance and love from the God she'd fallen in love with years earlier, she began reading the works of more progressive faith authors like Richard Rohr. Eventually, Erin found her way back to church, though not a church of the Catholic faith. She began attending a mainline Protestant denomination and was able to find hope and peace in those services. Ultimately, she realized that she may never be able to fit the nostalgic pieces of Catholicism back into her life the way they once were, but that didn't mean that she had to let go of her faith altogether. She was able to discover God in a new light and, in the process, find acceptance, love, and belonging just as she was.

Paula's biggest awakening after her transition was the realization of the amount of privilege that straight, white, cisgender men possessed—that she had possessed all her life as Paul—and that she no longer had now that she transitioned to Paula. It was shocking to her to experience firsthand just how much privilege men hold, and how equally unaware both men and women are of it. Yet it is all either of them have ever known. Learning about this gap in status and privilege, Paula has become a voice for gender equality in a way that not many other people can. She is among the small percentage of people who have lived both as a man and as a woman and who now experience these vastly different life perspectives and experiences. Paula has also regained a place in ministry. She is the pastor of preaching and worship ministries at a newly planted affirming church, and a sought-after speaker nationwide. Though the pain of her past is still recent enough to be fresh in her heart, her confidence in who God created her to be and of her much-needed place in this world are causing her to flourish and to thrive. And it is all because she listened to that still, small voice of God that called her toward a life of authenticity.

For us LGBTQ people of faith, fostering self-acceptance is as important as breathing. We must accept ourselves in order to move freely and confidently through the world. Being a minority is exhausting because it's not something from which you can ever take a break. It is always there. Loving ourselves and making sure we are physically, mentally, emotionally, and spiritually healthy are things we continually talk about throughout this book because they are so crucial to our ability to thrive. Over the next three chapters we discuss specific ways of fostering self-acceptance so that we can finally live and love ourselves the way God has unashamedly loved us from the very beginning.

TO THE PARENT OR ALLY

If you have children, whether they identify as LGBTQ or not, I highly encourage you to expose them to diversity from a young age. The LGBTQ community may not yet be reflected in your own family, but helping your children engage diversity of all kinds early on will help them be better adjusted individuals and feel more accepted in the world and at home as they grow older. Do your part to talk with your kids about these topics of diversity in your everyday conversations. Hearing these types of conversations take place teaches them that you accept and value all people and allows them to know that if they or one of their friends come out, your home will be a safe place for them to be accepted and loved, and to belong.

2

Claiming Hope

Reestablishing Your Worth as a Child of God and Fostering Self-Acceptance

When you discover your self-worth, you will lose interest in anyone who doesn't see it. They may accuse you of having a big ego or wanting someone who is perfect, but those are guilt and shame triggers. Love has no guilt and there is no shame in self-respect. If they mistake one for the other, it just means they don't have what you're looking for.

—Doe Zantamata

When I was a kid, I remember watching the 1993 version of *The Secret Garden* starring Kate Maberly. As a nine-year-old, I was enchanted by the idea that this forbidden key led her to a beautiful and secret world that was all her own. It was a safe place away from her pain where she could escape and be herself. I longed for a place like that. Growing up, I had a fantasy about having a secret door behind one of the pictures on my wall that I could crawl through and escape into my own secret hideaway. Of course, that would have been impossible considering that it was actually the wall where the fireplace vent ascended to the roof. But in my head, it was just a safe little cubbyhole to which I longed to escape. It's where my mind would take me when I felt the world closing in.

So when I saw *The Secret Garden* and the way that Mary Lennox was able to escape from the troubles of her childhood into this space of beauty and wonder, I was in awe. Though the garden was dead at first, the tender care she and her friends gave it made it come to life with rich color, elegance, and vibrancy. The day she opened that mossy, wooden door in the stone wall and entered into a garden fully alive was magical.

Diversity and beauty go hand in hand. The beauty of that garden came from the overwhelming variety in the flowers, plants, and colors—all in various stages of blooming and growth. If the entire garden was filled with red roses, it would be pretty, but its beauty would be one-dimensional. But when you have red roses and yellow sunflowers and pink tulips and orange marigolds and purple irises and blue hydrangeas and white daisies and bamboo and baby's breath and chrysanthemums and orchids and cottonwood trees and lilac bushes and lilies floating on the pond . . . when all these plants bloom and grow together, the beauty is not only captivating, it takes your breath away. The beauty is held in the diversity represented. When everything is the same, even if it's charming, it becomes boring rather quickly. But when diversity enters in, richness, warmth, and intensity take hold and cause us to feel alive.

As LGBTQ people, we're not unlike *The Secret Garden*. We often try to hide our *selves* behind a wall, locking the door to our heart, and hiding away the key so that no one can see who we really are. But by locking everyone out, we also keep everything in. Without tending and nurturing our souls, we slowly wither and die inside just as that garden did. Soon, weeds of shame and humiliation and disparagement begin to grow. We suffocate ourselves by denying our identity the ability to bloom, because we are afraid.

But when we are willing to open the door and give ourselves the gifts of self-acceptance, self-worth, love, hope, belonging, and value, then and only then will we be able to blossom into who we were meant to be.

Diversity isn't meant to be kept hidden behind a wall or under lock and key. It's meant to be shared with the world. In the closing scene of the movie, Mary says, "If you look the right way, you can see that the whole world is a garden." And indeed it is. We just need to find the courage to unlock the door to our heart, so that we can add our own richness and depth to the already very diverse, very textured, and very beautiful family of God.

One of my favorite quotes comes from Marianne Williamson. It's inspired me for over a decade and I hope it will now do the same for you:

> "Our deepest fear is not that we are inadequate.
> Our deepest fear is that we are powerful beyond measure.
> It is our light, not our darkness, that most frightens us."
> We ask ourselves, Who am I to be brilliant, gorgeous,
>   talented, fabulous?
> Actually, who are you *not* to be?
> You are a child of God.
> Your playing small does not serve the world.
> There's nothing enlightened about shrinking so that other
>   people won't feel insecure around you.
> We are all meant to shine, as children do.
> We were born to make manifest the glory of God that is
>   within us.
> It's not just in some of us; it's in everyone.
> And as we let our own light shine, we unconsciously give
>   other people permission to do the same.
> As we're liberated from our own fear, our presence
>   automatically liberates others.[1]

"We were born to make manifest the glory of God that is within us." I don't have any tattoos, but if I did, this would be close to the top of my list. Every time I read it, I am inspired to live more authentically, more bravely, and more fully alive. What if we did allow the glory of God to be manifest in us and through us? What if, by living authentically, we give another person the courage to do the same? What if, by facing our own fear, we are able to liberate another? We are children of God, each of us displaying a unique piece of God's splendor to the world. Without us being vulnerable and living as who we were meant to be (by hiding our secret garden), one less color is represented in the larger garden of God's diversity. But as each of us strives

to become more fully alive, we germinate those around us to grow more fully into their own beauty as well.

HONORING DIVERSITY

Diversity is such an important part of the family of God. We have no reason to fear or be intimidated by it. Rather, we should be inspired, in awe, and encouraged to celebrate the uniqueness that each of us brings to the family. Consider these three stories of diversity, out of the hundreds I've heard, from people I've met along this road of being an LGBTQ Christian. My hope is that as you read them you will feel beauty, experience wonder, and come to appreciate the unmatched splendor that each of us can offer in order to enrich the world around us.

A Beautiful Story of an Interfaith
and Intercultural Marriage

Ryannie grew up in an interfaith family. Her dad was Jewish, and her mom was Christian. From a young age, her parents encouraged her to believe in whatever faith felt right for her, so Ryannie didn't experience the fundamentalist upbringing that inhibits many LGBTQ people of faith. Unconfined and free to explore her beliefs for herself, Ryannie was able to develop her own faith from what her family modeled for her. But Ryannie was also born deaf into a hearing family, making her exposed to diversity from the time of infancy. So when Ryannie realized she was gay, coming out was challenging for her in different ways than for others. Introverted and shy, she preferred keeping the intimate parts of her life quiet. Although she had an uncle who also came out as gay and was largely supported by the family, Ryannie chose not to come out until after graduating from college. Her family was supportive, yet it still took time for Ryannie to comfortably identify as part of the LGBTQ community. Once meeting Erica and getting more involved in a group called Deaf Rainbow of Faith, Ryannie was able to come into herself and be more confident in her identity as a deaf, gay woman.

Erica grew up in a much more conservative home and culture in Houston. Not allowed to talk about her feelings growing up, Erica hid her sexual orientation and buried it deep within her while attending seminary and working in churches. Though privately she was aware that she was gay, she believed that if she just remained single, no one would ever need to know about her hidden identity. In time, the stress she harbored began to manifest itself physically and spiritually. As she moved further along in her ministry, Erica realized it was impossible to compartmentalize these two seemingly opposing parts of her heart. She knew that if she wanted to continue in ministry, she had to be honest about who she was, including the fact that she was gay. Being single or being in a relationship no longer mattered; being authentic about who she was at her core now took precedence. Knowing there were limited opportunities for people at the intersections of being a gay, female pastor, Erica began to grieve the loss of a dream that she thought could never be.

Once Ryannie and Erica met and began dating they took pride in the diversity of their relationship. Though they were both gay women of faith, Ryannie was Jewish and part of the Deaf community, while Erica was Christian and hearing. Their differences drew them closer to one another, teaching them the importance of communication, the value of not making assumptions because of their cultural differences, and the freedom of being able to ask clarifying questions in order to learn more about one another's experience, language, and religion. Though admittedly they experienced a bit of culture shock in their own relationship, it was something they leaned into for strength rather than something that drove them apart. Although they've found that their diversity often makes others uncomfortable (either because they are two women, or because they are an interfaith couple, or because Ryannie is deaf and Erica is hearing), these differences have challenged them to dig deeper into understanding even more about different groups and cultures, seeing everything as an opportunity for learning and growth.

Eventually, Ryannie and Erica married and Erica became the first openly gay lead pastor to be hired by a church in her denomination. Although the support of Erica's parents has been inconsistent, both of the women's families came for their civil wedding ceremony. They then had a formal wedding the following year with family and friends, which showcased all the beautiful diversity that they as a couple bring to the world.

A Courageous Display of Transgender Diversity

Chris grew up in the South always knowing he was different. Although he was biologically born a girl, Chris hated dresses and despised makeup and dolls. Jealous of the boys around him, he envied their bodies and the way they lived so freely. While Chris didn't have a name for what he was feeling, his gender dysphoria began at the age of four and Chris always hoped that someday he'd get to be one of the guys.

His parents were deeply involved in their faith community and held very conservative views when it came to the interpretations of the Bible. Because they were considered spiritual pillars among their peers, Chris was at church every time the doors were open. Suppressing his feelings in order to please God and his family, much of Chris's church experience was based on behavior modification rather than a real relationship with God.

Following high school and college, Chris pursued a graduate degree in biblical counseling by attending seminary. Secretly he hoped that by immersing himself in the study of the Scriptures, he could figure out what was wrong with him and rid himself of these conflicting emotions. He knew that if he told anyone about his identity, he would be hated and forced into reparative therapy. And because he was taught that emotions lie to you and can't be trusted, Chris found it easier to just shut down inside and feel nothing at all.

No matter how much Chris cried and prayed for God to change him, his prayers went unanswered. He couldn't get past the fact that, had he been biologically born a boy, everything would have been normal. But because he was anatomically born a girl, he could never live up to the preconceived ideas of what everyone expected a daughter to be.

Eventually, depression worsened into suicidal ideations and Chris knew that he needed to face his identity head on. With the passing of HB2 in North Carolina in 2016, Chris finally learned what it meant to be transgender. Having the vocabulary to identify himself made it easier to finally accept who he was. It felt less complicated for him to see himself as an FTM (female-to-male) transgender person (or as he thought of it, a "straight male") than to accept that he was a female attracted to women. In essence, it fixed the discord in his mind around being gay.

But that didn't mean he felt welcome to remain in seminary. Dropping out of school and for a long time following, Chris wanted to leave faith behind all together. It caused too much pain and was too exhausting to feel like he could never measure up. But in time, Chris realized that he needed his faith as much as he needed to be himself. Faith was an intrinsic part of who he was, and he just couldn't let it go.

Chris has been transitioning over the last couple years and feels like he passes in his innate gender about half the time, but still he struggles with feeling like people see him with one foot in each gender. He often uses poetry to express himself and educate people around him about the diversity he brings to the family of God.

A Story of Strength from a
Gay Asian Woman in the Military

My wife, Clara, is a first-generation Filipino immigrant. She was born in the Philippines and remained there as a toddler with her grandparents, while her mom and dad moved to

Hawaii ahead of the family to start a new life in the States. A full year passed before Clara was reunited with her parents in Hawaii. With her mom and dad hard at work to succeed in their new homeland, Clara grew up as a latchkey kid learning independence from a young age. Spending her afternoons involved in sports and athletics, she had no interest or time for boys. She also had no desire for things like makeup or frilly clothes. She didn't want to *be* a boy; she just didn't like all the feminine aspects that came with the typical expectations of being a girl. But Clara's strong-willed nature kept her from caring about measuring up to society's standards, and instead she marched to the beat of her own tomboy drum. She may not have known the word for it, but Clara instinctively knew she was gay from the time she was five and recalls being attracted to girls for as long as she can remember.

Although originally from a Catholic background, Clara's family later became involved in a fundamentalist Baptist church in Hawaii, making religion a strong part of her life. With that also came an intrinsic knowledge that being gay was unacceptable. So even though Clara already knew the truth about herself, she did what seemed like the only option, never telling anyone about her attraction to girls. Trying hard to please God with her life and praying for God to make her straight, she did all the right things in order to make herself acceptable to God. She attended InterVarsity, she pleaded regularly with God to fix her and promised anything in return, and she gave dating guys her best attempt, all in effort to cure her sexual orientation—but to no avail.

After high school, Clara attended an all women's college. With primarily females as her professors and campus staff, Clara learned leadership skills unequal to anything she could have learned in a coed institution. Without men to take the lead, women had more opportunities to rise up, analyze and solve problems, and take authority over situations. Embedded in the students was the notion that they were equipped and equal. But as much as that experience shaped Clara's character to be the strong, Asian female that she is, she continued to wrestle in the closet with her sexuality during her college years, which was only magnified when she fell in love with her resident adviser. Heartbroken when the feeling wasn't reciprocated, Clara retreated even further into the closet and began experiencing deep depression.

Spiraling downward into a pit of despair, Clara reached the point where she felt like suicide was her only option. If God couldn't fix her, she didn't want to live. Knowing that her dad was a gun owner, the day came when everyone was out of the house, and Clara decided she was done fighting. She knew exactly where her dad's guns and ammunition were kept and went to retrieve them with plans to end her life. But when the time came, she looked in all the usual places and there wasn't a gun or a bullet to be found anywhere. Even amid the frustration and isolation of the moment, Clara broke down, knowing that God had saved her life that day. She didn't know what the future held, but she knew her time was not yet up.

Pressing on and regaining the will to live, but still combating intense internalized homophobia, Clara put herself where she was certain her sexuality could not be seen or known; she enlisted in the U.S. Army. With the "Don't Ask, Don't Tell" (DADT) policy prohibiting discrimination or harassment toward closeted LGBTQ service members but barring openly LGBTQ personnel from military service, the choice for Clara was clear: she would stay in the closet and serve her country.

In time, Clara ended up resigning herself to the fact that she could never be with a man and instead found a Christian girlfriend. But still, her personal life was kept very separate from her professional life in the military. Four years into the relationship, her girlfriend cheated on her, launching Clara into a decade of anger and separation from God: "Why did you make me like this?" "What's the point of dating a Christian if they cheat on you like everyone else?" "Why would I want to go to church when everyone there tells me I'm going to hell?" She had come to the end of her religious rope and banished God to exile from her life.

It was years before Clara was able to reconcile her faith with her sexuality. But eventually, she found her way to an affirming church, which is where she and I met. While parts of her ethnic and cultural background still shape who she is, her faith continues to be deconstructed and reconstructed into one that portrays a much more loving, embracing, and inclusive God. Much of that process has been one that we've shared together as we've learned, read, listened to those around us, and grown in our spiritual journey of faith.

Being at the intersection of so many minorities (Asian, gay, female, and immigrant), has challenged and stretched Clara in many ways, but it has also caused her to be a woman of strength, courage, and integrity. She speaks her mind, she is quick to admit her mistakes, and she stands up for what she believes is right—all qualities that made me fall in love with her. As we continue our journey of marriage together, we sharpen one another and care for one another, and the love we share challenges us to bring all of ourselves to the relationship so that we can live together—successes and failures, strengths and flaws—from a place of vulnerability and authenticity, and know that we always have a place to belong with each other.

YOU BELONG

No matter your background, your race, your religion, your ability or disability, your gender identity, or your sexual orientation, you belong in the family of God. We are all designed uniquely and we all bring something different to share. One ability or skin color should not be elevated over another, nor should being cisgender and straight be the coveted cultural norm. We each should embrace who we are to the fullest, ground ourselves in our identity, and boldly display it to the world around us. Don't shrink back, don't hide who you are, and don't convince yourself into believing the lie that you are unacceptable because of [fill in the blank], or that you would love yourself more if you were just _____ [straight, cisgender, thinner, more muscular, etc.]. Comparing ourselves to the world around us only diminishes the beauty we possess. There is nothing unique about uniformity. Only by displaying and embracing our skin color, our bodies, our abilities, our ethnicity, our faith, and our LGBTQ identity will we become fully alive. And once you come alive, nothing can hold you back. You will be unstoppable.

FOSTERING SELF-ACCEPTANCE

Fostering self-acceptance is one of the hardest things for us as LGBTQ Christians to do. With years of conservative theology playing in our heads, it is hard (and takes time) to erase those tapes and build a new library of affirming beliefs about ourselves. You must give yourself the permission you need to be where you are and to allow yourself to go through the process.

Some Tips for Loving Yourself

Release yourself from expectations
If you've grown up in the evangelical church like I have, you most likely put a lot of pressure on yourself to perform and measure up in order to make God and those around you happy. You may feel pressure to spend an hour in prayer and Bible study every day, or be at church every Sunday without fail, or fast at least one day a week to "pray your gay away." You need to let go and release yourself from all of that. Accepting an LGBTQ identity can be difficult for anyone, but even more so for those of us who feel the constant pressure to measure up and conform. The expectation is so high that we don't know how to stop.

In order to begin a new narrative for yourself, give yourself the grace to take space where it is needed. That may mean taking a break from church or not reading your Bible for a while if those things trigger you. Don't condemn or make yourself feel guilty for taking a break. God can and will meet you wherever you are. You don't have to be in a church to encounter God, and the Bible is not the only way that God speaks. If you are open, you can find God anywhere. It may be in a song on the radio, or in a quote someone posts on Facebook. Open your heart to listen, give yourself grace, and see what you discover—without standards or expectations.

Read books by affirming Christians

Start rewriting those tapes in your head by picking up a book by a progressive and affirming pastor, theologian, or teacher and listen to that person's understanding of life, God, and the Scriptures. You could choose from many authors, but a few I recommend are Richard Rohr, Sarah Bessey, Austin Channing Brown, Brené Brown, Rob Bell, and Rachel Held Evans. Each of these people are straight allies to the LGBTQ community and are doing amazing work on the forefront of spirituality, equality, and love for all of God's people.

Write yourself permission slips

In her book *Braving the Wilderness*, Brené Brown talks about writing yourself permission slips. Your permission slip may say something like, "Permission to take a break from church," "Permission to set healthy boundaries with non-affirming people," or "Permission to love myself." Whatever your heart needs, give yourself the grace to grant it that. Then write it on a sticky note and put it in a prominent place as a frequent reminder of the permission you've granted yourself.

Find at least one person with whom you can be completely yourself

Having at least one person with whom you don't have to filter what you say or do is liberating. It's especially important if you're dealing with internalized homophobia as discussed in the previous chapter, because internalized homophobia only thrives in isolation or non-affirming spaces. But when you bring your identity to the light in a place that is safe, just like shining a flashlight in the dark, the homophobia you feel toward yourself must immediately diminish in power.

Intentionally position yourself in affirming spaces

Putting yourself in affirming spaces is key, which is why the entire next chapter is dedicated to the importance of community. But for the sake of this section, know that finding an affirming space—whether an affirming church, an LGBTQ support group, or a therapist's office—is vital to being able to accept yourself. The more you are around people who affirm you, the more you will be able to affirm yourself. Support combats fear and self-degradation, causing you to feel less isolated and more supported in your journey.

Remember that being LGBTQ is a strength, not a weakness

Sometimes all we need is a paradigm shift in the way that we view ourselves or our situation. Recognizing your identity as a strength that brings character and diversity to who you are, rather than a weakness that makes you a misfit, can help you tremendously in the way you view yourself and the way you move through the world. Begin to affirm your identity as a valuable part of who you are and allow your identity to blossom and grow.

Find a role model

Look into the LGBTQ Christian community and find someone who can be a role model for you. Whether it is someone you know personally or someone you look up to from a distance, having someone you can glean wisdom from will help you realize that you can be an LGBTQ Christian and live the happy, fulfilling life you've always dreamed of. There are a growing number of LGBTQ Christians to learn from, and many of them are doing amazing work in the fight for equality.

Hold on to your dreams

Just because you are LGBTQ doesn't mean you can't get married (thanks to President Obama), or that you can't have biological children (thanks to medical science), or that you can't be in ministry ever again (thanks to progressive Christians). The dreams you had all your life may be packaged or played out a little differently with an LGBTQ identity, but most of them can still be accomplished thanks to the amazing people who have fought for our rights for so many years. Just because you're LGBTQ does *not* mean all is lost. You can still grab hold of your dreams and chase after all that you've ever wanted. Don't let this hold you back just because others think you don't belong. You *do* belong, and the world needs *you* to rise up and shine.

As you move forward in your journey of accepting yourself, let go of the shame you carry, hold on to hope, and love yourself exactly as you are. Fostering self-acceptance will propel you forward and help you embrace the many amazing things that are in store for you ahead.

TO THE PARENT OR ALLY

Accepting oneself as an LGBTQ Christian is one of the most challenging pieces of moving forward into a hopeful future. Your loved one *must* believe they are loved and accepted by God in order to embrace themselves and keep their faith. If they remain in the belief that God hates them or looks down on them for who they are, they will either continue to hate themselves, leave the faith altogether, or possibly even head in the dangerous direction of trying to end their life. They need *you* to be the embodiment of Jesus' unconditional love toward them. Speak life, love without strings attached, and whenever possible, remind them of their place in the family of God by including them in your family and life. I promise you, it will make *all* the difference.

3

We Need One Another

Building an Affirming Community

We are each of us angels with only one wing, and we can only
fly by embracing one another.

—Luciano De Crescenzo

I never played with Barbie dolls as a kid, but I knew what
they were—small plastic representations of what a woman
was supposed to look like. With a tall, slim body, blonde
hair, and blue eyes, Barbie was the model of perfection. I, on
the other hand, was none of those things. I was big-boned,
I had brown hair and hazel eyes, and I can't ever remember
a time in my life where I felt thin. The one thing I did have
in common with Barbie was the ability to wear a perpetual
smile.

No one ever told me directly that's what I was supposed
to do. I just knew. I copied the Christian women around me
whom I looked up to as role models. Sitting and drinking tea,
they talked about Joyce Meyer and shared why they believe
"everything happens for a reason." In my youth, I didn't question it. It was normal. But as I moved into my teen years, I
began to take note of what was going on around me. In my
ultraconservative environment, I noticed that outwardly, the
people I interacted with did all the right things—they went
to church, they homeschooled their children, they led Bible
studies, they went on mission trips, they fasted on a regular

basis, they acted like they had it all together and were always happy—but they were never *honest* with each other. I remember thinking to myself, *This isn't authentic community. I feel like I'm trapped in the masquerade ball from* Phantom of the Opera.

They called it being "blessed" or claiming the "joy of the Lord" as their strength. They used prayer, trusting God, and additional faith as their tools for handling any and every situation. They seemed perpetually happy, but they weren't *real.* Then I realized, perhaps I never liked Barbie dolls for the same reason that I struggled to connect with people: they were fake.

Even as I took part in young adult accountability groups that were said to make us more like Christ and strengthen our spiritual walk, it felt like a big facade. No matter what group I joined, the confessions that came from the women around me were things like slipping up on their diet or failing to spend an hour in Bible study and prayer every day that week. I thought to myself, *Either these women are seriously superficial or I am way less spiritual than I thought, because calorie-counting was the least of my worries this week!* It seemed so trivial to me compared to the deep secrets I harbored.

Sitting and listening to each of these ladies' confessions, I scrambled for what to say when my turn came. I was simultaneously desperate for someone to truly know me and terrified to show anyone what was in my heart, especially those with a plethora of Christian clichés on their lips. My struggles that week weren't petty things like slipping up on my diet or losing my temper with a family member. The battles I wrestled with were the ones no one wanted to talk about: struggles of deep depression, intense anxiety, crippling mental health, loneliness, and cutting and other forms of self-injury. But those types of confessions made people uncomfortable. Not knowing what to do with information like that, they'd often just slap a Band-Aid on it by saying something like, "We will pray for you," or "Just trust God, and he will give you strength to overcome it." That made me feel even more alone than I did to begin with. Over time, I learned it was better to just keep those things to myself.

But as far back as I can remember, I deeply longed for someone to see behind the masked smile I'd been trained to wear. I was desperate for at least one person with whom I could show the unfiltered me. I wore the mask because it was expected of me; I danced because that is what happy people do, but deep inside I longed for more. I longed for people to stop hiding behind idealized masks of perfection. I longed for authenticity. I longed to have the freedom to be real. I'd fine-tuned how to play my part, but it was exhausting, lonely, and suffocating for my soul. Little by little, I felt like I was dying inside.

I lived the first twenty-seven years of my life behind that mask, and the death of my soul was drawing near. But as I reached the end of my rope and was now struggling with my own sexuality on top of everything else, I went out on a limb one last time and typed "gay affirming church" into Google in a final attempt to find authenticity and a beacon of hope for my soul. A church in Denver appeared in the search results. Perusing their website and feeling like it held potential, I took the risk of emailing the pastor and poured out my very broken heart to him. Almost immediately I received a very warm response, followed by an invitation to visit.

So the first weekend of January 2012, I drove from Colorado Springs to Denver to visit this church for the first time. My whole world had been turned upside down over the past few years when I unexpectedly fell in love with my female roommate. It was the one thing that was *never* supposed to happen. In the order of unforgivable sins, that was at the top. The words my parents spoke when they found out about it had silenced me for months: "Amber, don't *ever* tell anyone about this, because if you do it will ruin your reputation forever."

Bound to a secret that ate away at my soul, my coping mechanisms of self-harm returned, and I was convinced that the unacceptable combination of having sex outside of marriage and doing so with a woman, as opposed to a man, made me useless to God. I believed that no man would want me after losing my virginity to a woman. I was devastated by the disappointment I knew I had caused my family, and I felt I was an utter failure to God. My life became bleaker by the day. Darkness clouded my brain, and suicidal thoughts began to take hold. It was more than I could bear.

Driving the sixty-seven miles between my house in Colorado Springs and this church in Denver, I understood this action as my final attempt at trying to make sense of the mess in my heart. Somehow I mustered the strength to give hope one last shot. I was desperate for a reason to keep living, but I was also afraid that people might actually see me—and equally afraid that they might *not* see me. I longed to be seen but didn't know what the consequences of that might be. I had hidden for so very long. I longed to belong and to feel safe. I wanted to hope, but I was afraid to hope for fear that I'd be disappointed.

Arriving at the church and making my way into the sanctuary, I sat with both hope and fear in my heart, waiting to see which would triumph. As the congregation began its service, among the first things I heard were the words of their ethos, which are read at every gathering:

> Married, divorced, and single here, it is one family that mingles here
>
> Conservative and liberal here, we've all got to give a little here
>
> Big and small here, there is room for us all here
>
> Doubt and believe here, we all can receive here
>
> LGBTQ and straight here, there is no hate here
>
> Woman and man here, everyone can here
>
> Whatever your race here, for all of us grace here
>
> In imitation of the ridiculous love almighty God has for each of us and all of us, we choose to live and love without labels.[1]

Tears streamed down my face. For the first time in years, my soul felt hopeful, alive, and free—like it could breathe.

They saw me and knew me. In many ways, I believe these were the words my heart had longed to hear all my life. *Now,* this *is authentic community,* I thought. It was deeper than a mere superficial reality. It was inclusive, honest, raw, and real.

That was the day I found my people, the day my heart found a place to call home, the day I learned I could bring all of me to the family of God and didn't have to filter what I said when I walked through the church doors. That day became a defining moment for me that would carry me through the months and years to come.

I drove from Colorado Springs to Denver every Sunday for the next six months, watching as people interacted with one another before, during, and after church. The atmosphere of this church was different from those I'd known. There was a love, warmth, and authenticity in the air that made it unique and refreshing. Rather than putting a mask on when they walked into church, people seemed to be taking off their masks and leaving them at the door. People who had to hide who they were during the week to their family, friends, or bosses—or all of them—could come inside these church walls and feel safe, like they belonged.

This captivated my soul, and I immediately began working on building community by meeting new people, exchanging stories, and going to lunch with a group of church members after every service. Those lunch conversations were the first time in my life that I heard people talk about their love for God and their love for their same-sex partner or spouse in the same breath without any conflict in between. I met couples who'd been together ten, twenty, even thirty years. That was monumental for me in terms of normalizing what I was going through. It was the most beautiful thing I'd ever seen. Not only that, but they were honest about their struggles, open about the difficult parts of life, and didn't seem to be hiding anything. I'd longed to meet these kind of people all my life, and it revolutionized the way I viewed what was possible for my future, giving me hope for life out from behind the mask.

THE IMPORTANCE OF BUILDING AUTHENTIC COMMUNITY PRIOR TO COMING OUT

Building community prior to coming out is vitally important for several reasons. First, it will help acclimatize you to a new kind of normal. Meeting and spending time with healthy people who love God and are committed to their same-sex partner or spouse or are confident in their gender identity give you hope for what you can have in your own future. You need healthy role models to give you confidence for a happy, fulfilling future. Just because you're gay or bi or trans does not mean that you can't get married or have a family with kids if that is what you want. Options are available to you, but you need to be in a space that models those choices in a healthy manner.

Second, you need support. You could come up against an entire spectrum of roadblocks in the process of coming out. You don't want to be scrambling for support when those challenges come. Having a foundation in place will sustain you when the road gets rocky.

There are many different kinds of support, but a few things to look for in order to start building your own supportive community are as follows.

An affirming church
While connecting to your local LGBTQ center and other types of support groups and organizations can be helpful, connecting to an affirming church is critical because it addresses your need to be seen as an LGBTQ person as well as a Christian. In a world that often tells people you can't be both, you need a place where the two coincide to see the possibility for yourself. Being an LGBTQ Christian is a unique challenge that not all LGBTQ people face, and you need a safe place to bring all parts of you without having to segregate or compartmentalize.

A good therapist
We talk more about the value of therapy in the next chapter, but finding a licensed therapist who respects where you are in your faith journey as well as supports the discovery process of

your LGBTQ identity and how to integrate both into your life is extremely helpful. An understanding therapist gives you not only a confidential space to process but also the confidence and tools you need to move forward. While many therapists can help you with interpersonal struggles, I recommend finding one who specializes in working with LGBTQ people, if possible, particularly LGBTQ people of faith. If you're struggling to find a therapist in your area, The Christian Closet is a web-based resource that provides online therapy for LGBTQ people of faith.

A close friend
You should have one to three friends whom you can put on speed dial and know that you can call them anytime. Talk with those friends ahead of time and explain that, in the process of coming out, emotions might hit you unexpectedly and you will need support or a listening ear. Explain what kind of support is most helpful for you—suggestions, unconditional listening, prayer, and so on—and ask if they are willing to take on this role for you.

A pet/companion
Not everyone has three great friends to put on speed dial. Something I learned in my coming-out process that I previously underestimated was the power of a pet. Animals are an amazing reflection of God's love and can teach us so much. Not only that, but if taken care of and treated properly, their love is truly unconditional, which isn't true about most people. When I got Half Pint, my Shih Tzu–Maltese mix, prior to coming out, I had no idea how much strength she would lend me in the following years. Every time I walked through the door, she was excited to see me. She didn't care if I was gone eight hours or ten minutes. To her, it was the best part of the day. On my hardest days, just knowing that there was a heartbeat waiting for me when I got home made the days a little less lonely. Even the knowledge that she depended on me daily for the simplest things like food and water gave me a sense of elementary purpose. Taking her for a walk meant I went outside

for fresh air. Knowing she needed to be fed pulled me out of bed in the morning. Knowing she was there to cuddle with me while I slept made the nightmares a little less scary. Sometimes all we need is a little consistency and normalcy in our day coupled with some true unconditional love. If you're at a place in your life where you have the time and resources for a pet, a little bundle of fur could make all the difference.

A small group
Involvement in a small church group offers a great opportunity to build additional support. Attending an affirming church is a good first step, but you can often end up lost in the crowd if you're not intentional. Being a part of a small group lets you be seen. You get to know people, and they get to know you. Not only does this give people the opportunity to support you through your own process, but you'll be surprised at how much your helping others with your presence gives you strength you didn't know you had. Investing your time, energy, and resources into others and allowing them to invest theirs into you is a true sign of community.

A hotline
While all these tools are important and have a place, sometimes you can't predict when something is going to trigger you and your speed-dial friends aren't available. Maybe something has even come up involving one of them. Having a hotline number on hand and knowing someone is always available to talk can help give you a sense of peace when so many other parts of your life feel out of control. There's no shame in reaching out. In fact, one of the best things you can do for yourself is to gift yourself with the chance to be heard. If you're unsure of which hotline to call, a list of numbers is available in the Resources section of this book.

The most important takeaway is to start building your support system *now*. If at all possible, create your supportive community before you need it. If it is too late for that and you're already treading water, do what you can now to jumpstart a community for yourself and let people know of your need for support.

Looking back, I can say without a doubt that the support network I had through my church and other avenues of involvement before, during, and after coming out absolutely saved my life. I attended my new church in Denver for four months before I came out to my family. Three months after coming out, I moved to Denver to be closer to a body of support; it was that crucial for my survival. When I had next to nothing but knew I needed to relocate to Denver, a church friend lent me the money I needed until I could get on my feet. When I became really sick with pneumonia but didn't have health insurance or money to pay for a doctor, a friend from choir gave me the money and demanded I go. Years later when I had absolutely no family at my wedding but desperately needed to feel supported in the act of my marriage, my church family sat where my biological family should have been and stepped in to help fill the void.

Even today, my affirming community continues to support my wife and me as we deal with challenges that arise for us. The people in that community continue to be our chosen family and carry us when times get hard. They are our people, and you need to find your people too.

THE DIFFERENCE BETWEEN AN AFFIRMING CHURCH AND A WELCOMING CHURCH

A few years ago, my wife and I decided to visit a local sister church of the church in which I was raised. On our first Sunday there, the pastor happened to preach a sermon about their doors being open to everyone in the community. "Everyone is welcome," he said with enthusiasm from the stage. He went to extensive lengths to explain that no matter what your background or financial status, no matter where you lived or what "sin" you committed—whether you were a single mother or had been incarcerated or lived on the streets—you were welcome and belonged here.

My wife and I sat listening carefully to that list, but unsurprisingly heard no mention of the LGBTQ community. I knew this pastor and his wife from the parent church where we'd both been members. Following the service, I took a step of courage and raised the question. I wrote him an email, mentioning my background, my long involvement at our parent church, and my recent marriage to my wife. I asked him if he *truly* meant all were welcome or if his statement actually meant everyone except me.

He didn't remember me at first, but upon agreeing to meet my wife and me for coffee to discuss the matter, he remembered not only me but also my family very well. Our mutual connection to a former church world and memories we both shared softened his heart a bit, and the door for conversation seemed to open as we sat and dialogued about our faith journeys. He asked questions with a fairly open mind and seemed open to learning. Eventually he admitted that his church was rather neutral on the subject of same-sex relationships and that we would never hear him preach about it from the pulpit one way or the other. He wanted us to feel welcome in his church.

Then my real question came: "So if I wanted to join the worship team or lead a small group, would I be allowed to do that?" He paused and admitted he wasn't sure. No one had been gutsy enough to ask him that question point-blank before. He said he would pray about it, talk to the church leadership, and let us know.

Anyone who has been through a similar process at a church knows what the answer was. As at many other churches, we were "welcome" to attend, give our money, and volunteer our time, but not to lead. Leading as a gay Christian woman wasn't a risk they were willing to take or theologically support.

For some reason—perhaps longing, nostalgia, or stupidity—my wife and I decided to visit just one more time. The day we went was ironically the second part of a two-week sermon series on sex. The first sermon, which we had missed, had been on "Good Sex," and the week we showed up was (you guessed it) the discussion of "Bad Sex."

A knot began forming in my stomach from the moment I heard the title and continued to churn with every passing minute. I waited in fear and anticipation of what may come. Then the moment finally arrived. To my shock but sadly not my surprise, when offering examples of bad sex—including pedophilia, pornography, and incest—this same pastor with whom we'd just had coffee only weeks prior also listed homosexuality.

I wanted to stand up and walk out right then and there. My blood was boiling, and I immediately felt not only betrayed but very unsafe.

I left so deeply hurt that day. I was hurt because he told me to my face that we'd never hear him talk about this from the pulpit. I was hurt because I felt like we had established some kind of rapport and respect for one another, yet he still listed my beautiful and pure marriage to my wife as defiled. I was hurt because I felt betrayed once more by someone who knew my history and my family, and with whom I shared years of mutual memories. I was disturbed and disheartened.

I ruminated on that sermon for weeks. Finally, I felt like I needed to tell this pastor how his words affected me. After sending an email that vulnerably revealed my pain and heartache, his response was short and simple: he wasn't going to apologize or alter what the Bible clearly stated as truth. That was it.

I could never bring myself to walk through the doors of that church again.

Because of stories like this and the heartbreaking experiences of so many other LGBTQ people in church spaces, it is vitally important to know the difference between simply being welcome in the church and being fully affirmed as equal in the body of Christ. Many churches say, "All are welcome here," but what they really mean is that you are welcome to attend service, give your tithe, and maybe even volunteer in a "lesser" role like hospitality, but when it comes to serving in a leadership capacity or getting married, they draw the line. This stance is damaging for so many LGBTQ people because it causes us to feel subhuman or less-than simply because of our sexual orientation or gender identity.

If you choose to engage in a welcoming but not affirming church because you feel God is asking you to stay and be a light, at least know ahead of time where the church stands theologically and what their doctrine is concerning LGBTQ people so that you're not hurt or surprised down the road. Some people feel called to stay in those situations; many of us do not. Choosing to engage in a non-affirming faith community can be deeply damaging to your soul in the long run. What's more, choosing to *not* engage in a faith community that is damaging to your soul is completely right and healthy. God would not ask you to stay in a harmful place. You have every right to protect your heart and walk away if staying is at all detrimental to your physical, psychological, emotional, or spiritual health.

HOW TO FIND A SAFE AND AFFIRMING CHURCH COMMUNITY TO FEED YOUR SOUL

With the launching of Church Clarity in 2017, we are fortunate to now have a way of knowing exactly what a church's policies are in regards to LGBTQ inclusion. On its website, ChurchClarity.org, you can search by region or denomination and find churches in your area that have been scored. Each church listed has undergone a complete review by one of Church Clarity's advocates and, based on its policies, placed in categories along the lines of Non-Affirming, Undisclosed, Unclear, Actively Discerning, and Clearly Affirming. You can review what each rating means, and if you are curious about a certain church you don't see listed, you are able to submit the church's name for review.

Church Clarity advocates for transparency of church policies regarding LGBTQ inclusion, and I believe their work is vitally important for the health, well-being, and spiritual growth of LGBTQ Christians. It's important because the difference between "welcoming" and "affirming" matters—a lot. It marks the difference between "you are equal here" and "you are welcome despite the fact that you're flawed." It marks the difference between "we celebrate who you are" and "we want to fix who you are." And it also marks the difference between "we embrace you" and "we love the sinner, but hate the sin." We need to understand a church's policies so that we as LGBTQ people know what to expect before we walk through the door—so that we feel safe and can protect ourselves from additional spiritual trauma. We need to feel equal and included—like we belong.

BUT WHAT IF MY AREA DOESN'T HAVE ANY AFFIRMING CHURCHES?

You may live in an area that does not yet have an affirming church nearby, or perhaps there are affirming churches but not in the same faith tradition in which you were raised. If that is you, know first that you are not alone. Many people are still searching for that safe home church community where they feel fully embraced. Slowly, more churches are coming out as fully affirming, but it is taking time. If you don't have an affirming faith community from your denomination in your area, you have some options.

Consider trying a new denomination
A new faith tradition may be different than what you are used to. It may stretch you a bit, but it may also refresh you. This is the perfect time to open yourself up to the insight and richness provided by other denominations or faith traditions that are not your own. You may even find it freeing and liberating to worship God in a new and different way. Allow yourself space to grow and be open to learning something new.

Get online and plug in with some of the resources listed in this book

Connect with others virtually and build an online faith community. Social media gives us the unique opportunity to connect with like-minded people all over the world. The more you join groups on Facebook and follow like-minded people on Twitter and Instagram, the more those websites's algorithms will connect you to the resources you are looking for. Start by following some of the people listed in the Resources section of my website at AmberCantorna.com. I try to keep an updated list of bloggers, organizations, books, podcasts, and musicians that I feel could be helpful to those on this journey.

Attend a progressive Christian conference

A growing number of progressive Christian conferences each year provide safe places for everyone, including LGBTQ people, to learn and grow in faith together. Some of these conferences are the Q Christian Fellowship Conference, the Why Christian? Conference, the Evolving Faith Conference, The Reformation Project Conference, and the Wild Goose Festival. Being in an affirming space, even if only for a weekend, can be immensely encouraging and uplifting for your soul.

Start a small faith community of your own

Advertise a small group or support group gathering in your home, at your church (if they will let you), or at a local coffee shop. If you create something that doesn't already exist in your area, people will find you. Most likely, they want a safe community just as badly as you do.

Community is one of the key components that will help you thrive through your coming-out process. Begin making a plan now of how to build your support network so that it will be as strong and rich as possible when your coming-out time arrives. You'll need them to lean on, and if you choose the right people, they will actually want the opportunity to be there for you.

TO THE PARENT AND ALLY

If you are a parent or ally of an LGBTQ person, support them by helping them find a safe faith community. Offer to help them research affirming churches in their area and go with them the first few times they attend. Going to a new church can be intimidating for anyone, but for the LGBTQ person who has already been traumatized by harmful theology in church spaces, walking into a new community can feel extremely vulnerable for them. Lending your support can give them the strength they need to start on a new path of spiritual healing and wholeness.

FOR THE CHURCH LEADER

If you are a church leader in an affirming church, go to Church-Clarity.com and have your church rated and added to their list of clearly affirming churches. As the number of LGBTQ Christians continues to grow, the need for more affirming churches is vital for the success and health of our diverse believers. Make sure they know they are safe, valued, and included in the body of Christ where you worship.

4

How Do I Know If I'm Ready?

Preparing to Come Out

And the day came when the risk to remain tight in a bud was
more painful than the risk it took to blossom.

—Anaïs Nin

One of the most common questions people ask me is, "How
do I know when I'm ready to come out?" It's a scary and vulnerable subject. It feels as if your entire future hangs in the
balance of that one, huge, overarching question: *Am I ready?*

No one but you can answer the question of when you are
ready to live your full truth. But as you prepare yourself for
coming out, you can use several tools as a holistic approach to
examining your life and knowing if you are indeed ready. In
reality, coming out doesn't just affect one part of our life; it
affects all parts of our life because our sexuality is an essential
element of how we live, view, and experience the world. Therefore, all parts of you should be in alignment before you make
the leap of coming out.

AM I MENTALLY READY?
THE IMPORTANCE OF THERAPY

For far too long, mental illness and psychotherapy have
received a bad rap from the Christian community. We are told
to pray more, to memorize Scripture, to trust God. We believe

the lie that if we are weak, the reason is that we do not have enough faith. Ultimately, we are convinced that the sole way to healing and wholeness is through religious rituals like Bible reading, accountability groups, and fasting retreats. Many of us spend years trying to fix things that are not within our power.

From as young as my early elementary years I can remember trying to measure up to the ultimate Christian standard of perfection. It was an impossible task. The fear that because my obsessive-compulsive tendencies and anxiety weren't subsiding meant that I wasn't trying hard enough caused me great distress. I began harming myself as punishment and repenting hundreds of times, asking forgiveness for things that I now know I couldn't control. But because therapy and mental illness were taboo, I didn't receive the help I needed until my late teen years when the symptoms were much more severe. Even then, it would be almost another decade before I received the help I really needed—outside the Christian circle—to recognize that the root of much of my depression, anxiety, and self-harm stemmed from my closeted sexual orientation.

While I do believe that faith and positive thinking can influence our outlook on life, as Christians we've convinced one another to ignore the warning signs when our body is telling us that something is wrong. We've created so much shame around mental illness that many of us wrestle in isolation.

Unfortunately, isolating yourself in the face of mental illness is easy because the illness is often not visible to others. If you break your foot and are in a cast, everyone knows, and therefore you receive more sympathy and care. But for the invisible illnesses we face—physical or mental—we can conceal them from others, but concealment doesn't change their reality or validity.

I deal with chronic pain on a daily basis from an injury in 2013 that did permanent damage to the ligaments around my lower spine. Some days my pain is visible to others, and many days it is not. However, people treat me differently when I walk with a cane because they can see the evidence of my disability. But for those of us who so often wrestle in silence and isolation, we need to learn to verbally advocate for our needs, especially when it comes to our mental health.

The time has come for us to recognize mental illness for what it is: an illness, just as any other part of our body has the capability to malfunction. Our bodies are not perfect; they are human. The chemicals that affect our brain are no different than those affecting our blood pressure, circulation, or thyroid. Just like we would take a medication if our doctor told us we have the potential for blood clots, we also need to be open to taking medication when the doctor tells us that our brain chemicals are out of balance. There is no shame in doing so. And just like our bodies require physical therapy sometimes to recover from an injury, at times our mind and soul require mental therapy or counseling to help them recover. There is no shame in that either.

Therapy with the right person can be an extremely helpful step in guiding you toward healing and wholeness. But you should know a few things when looking for and choosing the right person to counsel you.

Make sure the person is a licensed professional
A lay counselor or a Christian with counseling training is not the same as someone who has studied and devoted time and education to the field of therapy. Be sure they have the letters to back up their title and ask about their credentials if you are unclear. Many therapists have a special focus in their field. It may be marriage and family therapy, PTSD, or addiction. Find out about their specialized fields and make sure they have the experience and training necessary to meet your individual needs.

Make sure the therapist supports your desire for reconciling your sexual orientation or gender identity with your faith
I cannot stress enough how vitally important this matchup is to your success. If you pair with a religiously minded therapist intent on changing or fixing you, or using any version of

reparative therapy—even a therapist like Erin's who clearly had his own issues with homophobia—you will inevitably leave way more conflicted, hurt, and confused than you already are. *That is not what you need.* You must find a therapist who honors all parts of you. Therapists don't have to share your faith, but they do have to respect it; they most certainly need to respect who you are as an LGBTQ individual. The best-case scenario is to find a trained therapist who specializes in helping people reconcile their faith with their sexual orientation or gender identity.

Make sure the therapist is right for you and don't be afraid to ask questions

Choosing the right therapist from among the many out there can feel daunting and overwhelming. Finding one who either works with your insurance or on a sliding-scale fee—a reduced fee for clients based on income or ability to pay—can be key to accepting that you can afford this investment over the long term. Also, feeling like the therapist understands you, has experience with therapy involving the struggles you're facing, and is someone you can trust are also vital elements to the client/therapist relationship. If you don't trust your counselor, you are unlikely to open up about what you are really feeling, in which case counseling is a moot point.

The first time you meet a therapist, don't be shy about going with a list of questions. After all, they will have plenty of questions to ask you during the first session. View your first appointment as a test run or interview and decide at the end if you want to schedule another appointment. Also, don't be afraid to see several counselors before deciding; it is no different than seeking a second opinion from a doctor for a medical need. When I needed to have foot surgery, I saw four different surgeons before I decided who would cut my foot open. Make sure you are comfortable and, above all, feel safe with the person counseling you. If you don't, find someone else.

Don't let the stigma of counseling hold you back from being your most authentic and alive self. Counseling was the first place I felt safe enough to bring together the seemingly opposing worlds of my faith and my sexual orientation. It helped me navigate the conflicting emotions I felt inside and come to a place of fully accepting myself as the beautiful, gay, Christian woman that I was designed to be. Therapy can do that for you too.

AM I PHYSICALLY READY? THE IMPORTANCE OF SAFETY AND INDEPENDENCE

In the midst of all the anxiety and pent-up emotions that accompany getting ready to come out, it is easy to forget some really practical things. Your safety is of the utmost priority when thinking about timing. Many safety issues have to do with your age and season of life. If you are in your thirties, for example, the experience will be different than if you are a teenager; if you are in college, it will be different than if you are in your fifties or sixties. I have met people from every imaginable age group, but regardless of life experience or demographic, you need to ask yourself some of the following questions to gauge your safety level for coming out:

— Do I have a stable job with reliable income?
— Do I have my own health insurance, or is a spouse or parent carrying that for me?
— Do I have or can I afford my own cell phone, electricity, and running water?
— Do I have a vehicle with the title in my name? Do I have or can I afford my own car insurance?
— Is there any chance I will be kicked out of my home once I come out? If so, do I have a backup plan of a friend or relative who will let me live with them, or do I have the financial means to afford my own living space?

—Do my parents or another relative or spouse pay for my college tuition or school loans? Can I assume that responsibility myself if it is cut off? What kinds of scholarships or grants might I be qualified to receive?

—Does coming out pose any threat of physical harm from the people I currently live with?

—Does one of my parents or close relatives or loved ones have a terminal illness? If so, is this something I feel is important that they know before they pass, or is it better, based on our relationship, that I wait to reveal my sexuality or gender identity until after they've gone?

—If I am married with children, do I have a strong case to get at least partial custody of my kids?

Some of these questions are no doubt sobering and very difficult. You may not want to think about or face them. I understand that the frustration and fear you experience just by reading this may cause you great anxiety. The unfortunate reality is that, in our society, the questions above are still very legitimate concerns in relation to coming out. If you are a teenager or still in college, these are most likely going to apply more to you. If you are in your mid to late twenties or thirties, chances are you are more financially independent and have your own living situation apart from your nuclear family, but that is not always the case. You may also be coming out later in life after having already been in a mixed-orientation marriage, and that comes with its own myriad of practical complications.

If you are able to read through this list of questions and feel pretty solid when it comes to your physical and financial living arrangements, that is a huge check mark off the list and will set you ahead in terms of being ready. If you read through this list and feel like a lot of those things are still out of your control, you have a good starting place for preparing. Try to not get overwhelmed; instead, begin to formulate a plan. You will not be able to control everyone's reaction to your coming out, but you can prepare for it.

AM I READY SPIRITUALLY?
THE IMPORTANCE OF THEOLOGY

As we move down the checklist of our holistic approach to coming out, theology plays a big part for many of us from an evangelical or more conservative Christian background. For me, it was paramount that I resolve the conflict between what I'd been taught and what I was feeling and experiencing deep inside my soul.

I was taught that homosexuality was an abomination; gay people were a threat to society and were sexually loose heathens who had turned their backs on God and were destroying the family unit; they were partiers and drunkards and pedophiles . . . and the list goes on. We didn't even give them the dignity of labeling them as LGBTQ. We just called them "homosexuals" or "perverts" or "the gays." Derogatory slurs and gay jokes were only secondary to the underlying understanding that this group of people was among the dirtiest and most defiled sinners of all. We "loved" them from a distance. We prayed for them. But we would never actually associate with them. What would people think? What would happen to our reputation? Would it rub off on our children, or on us?

These types of thoughts cause the internalized homophobia we addressed in chapter 1. To break that cycle of destruction, we need to reject the spoon-fed theology of our youth that forbids us from questioning and begin to look at the Scriptures for ourselves with fresh eyes. As Philippians 2:12 says, "Continue to work out your salvation with fear and trembling" (NIV). This doesn't mean to actually be afraid for your salvation, but rather to revere Scripture enough that you give it the consideration and care it deserves in order to understand it correctly.

As with Isaac from our opening chapter, we need to come to a new understanding of God and change the framework we use to view and understand the Bible. To do that, we need to understand the culture, history, and time in which the Bible was written to fully understand what the biblical passages that seem to reference same-sex relationships actually mean. Thankfully, some wonderful biblical scholars and theologians have done this research in recent years and written about it. I recommend *Changing Our Mind* by David Gushee and *Unclobber* by Colby Martin as some of the most accessible resources out there on the subject; they offer a solid starting place for this conversation. If you have already read those and want a more academic approach, you can visit my website, AmberCantorna .com, for additional resources.

Wherever you are on your theological journey, that's where you start. Pick up a book and begin to read with an open mind. There are plenty of resources available to you, but you will never be able to fully accept yourself if deep down you still believe that God hates you and is sending you to hell for all eternity. Do the work needed to reform your theology. You won't regret it.

Going on this journey may require that you distance yourself for a while from your evangelical church or conservative family and friends. You already have so much going on in your mind that you don't need additional voices to complicate your process further. Sometimes creating space to silence those condemning voices ends up being the very thing that sets us free. Ultimately, you need to separate what you learn of God personally from what people tell you or do to you in the name of God. The difference between the two isn't always easy to decipher if you have a myriad of voices trying to talk to you on God's behalf. Quiet those voices, glean from the wisdom of more progressive biblical scholars, listen to the voice of God yourself, and let your soul find rest.

AM I READY EMOTIONALLY? THE IMPORTANCE OF STRENGTH AND COMMUNITY SUPPORT

Discussing more progressive outlooks on God, Scripture, and sexuality leads me to my final point on the holistic inventory of your soul. As we covered in chapter 3, plugging into an affirming community is extremely important. Developing a strong support system in whatever form works for you will help you greatly in the months and years to come. If you build this support system and your family ends up embracing you when you come out, that is fantastic; you've just gained a bunch of new friends with whom you can celebrate. But if your family responds negatively and your relationship with your parents, siblings, or relatives becomes strained or severed, you will need this community of support to be your family of choice. They will lend you strength when yours runs out, and they will hold you up when you feel you can't stand. Invest time in building those relationships, in deepening them, and in fostering them in mutual ways so that you are confident that, regardless of what happens when you come out, you have people who are in your corner.

You never need to feel alone. As isolated as you may feel, online communities, private Facebook groups, hidden meetings on campus, and national conferences for LGBTQ Christians all provide places where you can meet people, build a supportive community, and be encouraged to thrive as the amazing human being you are. Once you reach out and make yourself known, you will realize that a whole sea of people are on this journey with you.

Checking each of these four categories off of your holistic soul inventory and knowing that you are mentally, physically, spiritually, and emotionally ready will help build your courage and confidence as you prepare to come out. If you've gone through counseling and know who you are, if you've become financially independent and have a stable living situation, if you know what you believe theologically, and if you have a community of support ready to walk with you through your process, you will feel more capable, strong, and equipped than if you don't take that holistic approach. Your goal, while you can't control the outcome entirely, is to have the least amount of aftermath and need for damage control as possible. Once you have all the pieces in place, you will feel much more grounded to weather whatever storm may come.

In the following sections, I answer some of the commonly

asked questions I receive about coming out. I also share with you, with their permission, the stories of some people who have reached out to me for support. For it is only in sharing our stories that each of us can feel less alone.

WHAT IF I AM FEELING PRESSURED TO COME OUT?

Jeremy didn't have many friends growing up. Struggling to fit in, he invested much of his spare time as a teen in the children's and youth ministries at his local church. Soon, Wednesdays and Sundays became the highlight of Jeremy's week. He loved working with the kids and helping them find their place of belonging. He found a sense of purpose in being a small group leader, helping with summer camps, and assisting in Sunday school classes. It was a way for him to give love to those who, like him as a young boy, longed for a positive role model. The love that was reciprocated back to Jeremy made him feel alive, like he was making a difference.

But when Jeremy came out to his parents as gay, his role in ministry came to an abrupt halt. His father, who worked in law enforcement and operated under the myth that all gay men are pedophiles, informed Jeremy that he felt a moral and legal obligation to tell the children's pastor that Jeremy was gay. Terrified of the consequences and knowing he was not yet ready, Jeremy begged his father not to out him to the church. But forcing Jeremy's hand, his father required Jeremy to call the pastor and tell him the truth. Just as he feared, Jeremy was asked to step down from children's ministry, and this import-ant and meaningful chapter in his life ended. Jeremy was devas-tated. He lived for those kids, and now the thing Jeremy loved most was taken away from him. The fiery passion in his heart dwindled to ash, and over the next few years Jeremy ended up leaving behind not only the church but Christianity as well.

This is the perfect example of why you should never have to come out due to peer or parental pressure. Just because you come out to one person does not mean you have to come out to everybody. If you have a story like Jeremy's where a parent or someone else in leadership has forced your hand or black-mailed you into coming out before you are ready, I am deeply sorry. That is something that only you should have the power to do, and you should be allowed to do it on your terms. Those people are not in your shoes. They do not know what it feels like to be LGBTQ in your family situation, church, job, or peer group. Only you know that.

In some situations, coming out happens outside of your control. But whenever possible, *take your time*. The decision to come out may affect only a small piece of your life, or it may drastically alter your life forever. No one else has to deal with the aftermath of coming out except for you. Do not cave into peer pressure just because your buddy at school is pushing you to come out or your cousin thinks it would be easier if your family knew. You will know when you're ready to come out. If you're not sure, then you are not ready yet. Trust your gut to lead the way.

WHAT IF SOMEONE ELSE OUTS ME BEFORE I'M READY?

When Brendon was eighteen, he had his first boyfriend. Although he'd known he was gay from the age of ten, Brendon kept quiet about his sexuality because he was raised in a Christian home with a father who taught at a Christian school. Growing up, he attended Bible camps each summer and later became a camp counselor, until one of the camp directors found out he was dating Mike. Once word got out that Brendon and Mike were a couple, they were both fired as camp counselors the week before camp was to start. The faculty told the young men that they needed to inform their parents themselves as to why they were let go. Without much time, Brendon and Mike both wrestled with how and what to tell their families. But before they could devise a plan, a vindictive and closeted mutual friend went to Brendon's family behind his back and told his parents and sisters that Brendon was gay and in a relationship with Mike. Outed and exposed before he was ready, the tension built as he prepared to face his father for the first time as his gay son. Once confronted, a myriad of questions ensued: "When did this start?" "How long has this been going on?" and "Did you pick this up at college?" were just a few of the darts thrown at Brendon's heart. Unready to be out and ill-prepared to answer such questions, the stress weighed on him as his dad informed Brendon of how homosexuality was destroying the world.

Thankfully, Brendon had Mike to lean on during this turbulent time, and the comfort of their love for one another carried them through the bumps ahead. But not everyone is so lucky. Brendon admits that had he been outed when he was single, the road would have been much more difficult.

It's cruel for anyone to out you before you are ready. The decision to tell someone about your sexual orientation or gender identity is very personal. If someone outs you, whether on purpose to be spiteful or by accident, you still have the right to do what you need to do to keep yourself safe. If you are not physically, emotionally, mentally, or spiritually in a place yet to handle the potential or actual collateral damage, it is okay to retreat back into the closet. If you are not feeling safe or stable enough to be out, there is no shame in doing what you have to do to survive. Your safety is *always* the ultimate priority. You have the right to come out on your own terms and when you are ready.

WHAT IF THE PERSON I'M DATING ISN'T OUT?

Kristen's relationship with Lily was the very definition of mountains and valleys. When Kristen began dating Lily, she thought they were both in the same place in regard to being out as gay Christian women. But as their relationship progressed, Kristen learned that Lily was still having an intense struggle to accept herself and know that God still loved her.

Lily was heavily influenced by her church and her community. Seeing Lily struggle to keep them appeased while simultaneously being unable to live an open life with Kristen was painful for them both. At times, Kristen felt like she was a secret that Lily kept; at other times, she felt like she was Lily's hidden blessing. The two of them had multiple conversations about ending their relationship, but each time they did, Lily would come back days later, pretending everything was fine.

With each round of self-questioning that Lily went through, Kristen also found herself beginning to question that which she thought she had already solidified. Her certainty of her place in God's family was replaced with uneasiness and doubt. It pained Kristen to watch Lily struggle, unable to come to a place of acceptance. And it hurt to watch Lily's church and closest friends not accept who God made her to be, but rather try to mold her as they wanted her to be. The pain in Lily's eyes was real, and her internal struggle was obvious. As someone who cared deeply for Lily, Kristen wanted to help her get to a place of peace and acceptance, but the more Kristen tried to help and encourage her down that path, the more distant Lily became.

Although Kristen loved Lily with an intensity she'd never felt toward anyone, Kristen eventually recognized that the journey toward self-acceptance was one that Lily would have to take on her own. No amount of pep talks, motivational quotes, reassurances, or support that Kristen could provide would speed up the process. Kristen finally realized that the greatest act of love was to set Lily free to embark on this journey for herself. Though it pained her to watch Lily hold herself back, Kristen had to take care of her own heart and move forward toward healing and wholeness for herself.

Many complications are present in a dating relationship in which one person is out and the other person isn't. If you are the one who is out, you may feel like you've done the work of being your authentic self while your partner is in a very different place in their process. The situation may seem okay at first, but over time it wears on you as you see your partner's pain from staying closeted. You may begin to take it personally and think that they don't love you enough to tell people about your relationship. You may even begin to question the authenticity of your relationship and feel like you are taking steps backward in your own journey of affirming your identity.

If you are in a relationship like Kristen and Lily's, it can be difficult for you both. Many emotions arise in the coming-out process. If you are the one still in that process, you deserve the time it takes for you to be comfortable telling other people about your LGBTQ identity. If you are the one who is already out and waiting on your partner, you have a decision to make: either agree to be patient and supportive of your partner as they go through this process, or set them free, as Kristen did, to walk the path needed to get to where they want to be. You can't push someone out of the closet just because it makes you uncomfortable. You have to honor their process.

If your faith backgrounds and family experiences are different, understanding why coming out is so hard for your partner may be difficult. Perhaps your family was very accepting and the backlash of your coming out was minimal, but other people may literally lose everything by declaring who they are. If you're struggling to understand that perspective, seek to learn more about people with that upbringing and experience by reading, talking with other people from similar backgrounds, and asking your partner forthright questions to help broaden your understanding. Your love for them should naturally draw this curiosity out of you, and in turn you will grow to love them even more deeply and have even more compassion and understanding for their situation.

IS IT OKAY TO BE OUT TO SOME PEOPLE AND NOT OTHERS?

BeeJay felt like she was living in a game of Minesweeper. As a kid she played the game without any thought as to how it actually worked. But as she grew older, she realized that being gay felt just as unpredictable. With one wrong move, everything could be suddenly lost. Just like Minesweeper, the rules for coming out in the conservative Christian world are unclear, but BeeJay knew one thing for certain: if she made the wrong move, she could lose everything, and there is no reset button.

So instead, BeeJay chooses to live quietly and proudly among the LGBTQ community, knowing they hold her uniqueness as something to be celebrated. But when she inhabits the conservative world—in her job, her extended family, her volunteer work, and her guest lecturing—she simply chooses to say nothing at all. She won't lie if asked point-blank, but she doesn't choose to announce her sexuality either.

BeeJay has seen friends take the bold step of coming out, choosing a gray square on their Minesweeper board. She has also watched as the board blew up beneath people, stripping them of their responsibilities, friendships, and even families—often in the name of love.

For now, BeeJay is at peace with being who and where she is in this season of her life. She admits that she ponders taking the risk of making that irreversible move and coming out fully. Perhaps one day she will. But for now she rests in the fact that she is in control of the game and will play it when she is ready on her own terms.

Coming out can feel like an overwhelming and daunting game of Minesweeper, especially when you think about having to tell everyone you've ever known that you are LGBTQ. But the reality is, unless you plan to come out with a big announcement on Facebook or you post a YouTube video that goes viral, you do not have to come out to everybody at once.

Coming out doesn't happen overnight. Some people choose to do it in a matter of days or weeks; some people, like BeeJay, do it over the span of years. The only right answer here is what's right for you. When you feel comfortable, confident, and ready, start taking steps to come out.

Some people, like Kristen's partner, stay in the closet because they are afraid of what coming out would cost them. If that statement describes you, zoom out and take inventory of what your silence is costing you already. For many, staying in the closet—whether by force, circumstance, or choice—ends up causing more harm than being authentic. By repressing who you are, you carry a burden of shame, often without even realizing it. You fall prey to the lie that part of you is so repulsive that you can never show it to anyone. Once you believe that, you become engulfed in a myriad of negative emotions that can lead to depression, anxiety, anger, fear, and self-hatred, just to name a few. These feelings have to manifest somehow; depending on your coping mechanisms, they may present in any number of self-destructive ways. Harboring this degree of inner turmoil in isolation can lead to physical illness as well.

You are worth more than that. Honor your journey and yourself by moving forward, even if you take baby steps. Your fear won't completely go away, but you will know when you are ready. Listen to that voice. Like a caterpillar in its cocoon, you are going through a transformation. Eventually, that place where you've lived will become burdensome and tiring. You'll reach the point where you're ready to shed that cocoon and make your way out into the light like the beautiful butterfly that you are: unashamed and ready to soar.

TO THE PARENT OR ALLY

If you are a friend or family member of an LGBTQ person, it is easy to take your straight or cisgender privilege for granted and not realize the impact that coming out may have on your friend or family member's life. For some people, being outed can be a real threat to their physical safety. For others it may cost them their job or their position in ministry. If you truly love the person, you need to respect the journey they are on and where they are at in that journey. Be considerate of the fact that coming out is very difficult. They are working through a lot of things while simultaneously trying to live their life and figure out how their identity plays into who they are in the world. Don't pressure them to have it all figured out before their time. Be patient; they will come out when they are ready. It takes an incredible amount of courage.

5

Taking the Leap of Faith

Coming Out to Your Loved Ones

When you have come to the edge of all the light that you know
and are about to drop off into the darkness of the unknown,
faith is knowing one of two things will happen: there will be
something solid to stand on, or you will be taught to fly.

—Patrick Overton

About a year before I came out to my family, I came across a black-and-white photo of a man who had strung a tightrope across Niagara Falls. He walked the tightrope back and forth, pushing a wheelbarrow out in front of him as he went. Naturally, it attracted a crowd. One day he addressed an onlooker who stopped to watch. "Do you think I can do it?" he asked the man.

"I know you can do it," the man replied. "I've seen you do it a dozen times."

The tightrope walker responded, "Then get in the wheelbarrow."

I first shared this story in my memoir, *Refocusing My Family*, but feel it is also worthy of sharing here. For those of us who come from conservative, religious backgrounds—especially evangelical circles—getting in a wheelbarrow to ride a tightrope across Niagara Falls is exactly what coming out can feel like. It's a huge risk and often one that holds a high chance of not turning out well.

For a full year before I came out to my family, I kept that picture taped to my fridge. It haunted me daily. Every time I

looked at it, I had to ask myself, *Do I trust God enough to met-*
aphorically get in the wheelbarrow and come out to my family? I
had never been more terrified in my life. The outcome was so
uncertain.

I grew up in a very certain world. My dad worked in a
prominent position at Focus on the Family, and my mom was
both the homemaker and the primary homeschool teacher to
my brother and me. My mornings started with family devo-
tions over breakfast at 7 a.m. My dad was home by 5:15 p.m.
every night, and my mom always had dinner on the table. After
dinner, we often memorized Scripture together. Church was
on Sunday mornings and Awana, an evangelical program for
children and youth, on Wednesday night. I had the coveted
Christian upbringing and the epitome of what's considered a
godly family. Life was scheduled, predictable, and safe.

We believed we were the chosen ones—God's elite. Instead
of doubt, we had certainty; instead of questions, we had biblical facts (or the literal interpretation of the Scripture); and
instead of wondering, we had prayer for wisdom and discern-
ment. With little wiggle room for examination outside what
we were taught from pastors, small group leaders, and Beth
Moore Bible studies, there weren't many shades of gray. Everything fell into a category of right or wrong, pleasing to God or
sinful, a choice that enhanced your relationship with God or
drew you farther away. Certainty was comfortable and easy,
creating boundaries by which we lived.

But this certainty came with a price tag. Our list of rules and
regulations of how to live and love others forced us not only to
exist within a very confined space but also to put up a facade.
The tiniest bit of doubt or unbelief was seen as weakness.
Although it wasn't overtly stated, the underlying principle was
that if you had enough faith and your trust in God was suffi-
cient, you should have your crap together (using the alternative
word for "crap" was not considered godly). Of course, no one
really has *all* their crap together, so instead we just pretended
like we did. We hid the broken pieces of our lives behind a
happy smile or an "I'm blessed" response when asked how we

were doing. If people didn't see our mess, then hypothetically, it didn't exist.

While simultaneously forcing us to hide our true selves, this also caused a level of judgment when it came to our fellow believers. If they were going through a difficult time or experiencing hardship, we first took pity on them and then concluded that it was most likely due to a lack of faith—that is, certainty. Struggle was evidence of weakness, so we committed to praying for them. In essence, *we* had this Christian thing figured out and *they* were still working on it. Everything was black-and-white, right or wrong, good or bad. We had all the answers. We were *certain*. Judging the lives of others was so easy with these formulas we possessed.

That is, it's easy—until that person experiencing hardship becomes us. When something unexpected happens in our life—a diagnosis, the loss of a child, a divorce, or the discovery of an LGBTQ identity—we begin to view life differently. Suddenly things aren't as black-and-white as they seemed. At first, we often put ourselves under the same scrutiny that we would others:

—What did I do wrong?
—Why can't I fix this?
—Maybe I really don't have enough faith.
—I promise I'll try harder, God, if only [fill in the blank].

We beg and bargain with God to take away the pain so that our certain and sure footing can be restored. But we've completely missed the point. *A belief system based on certainty doesn't really require any faith at all.* If we have everything figured out—if we have all the answers—why do we need faith?

Faith and certainty aren't intended to mix, as those of us in Christian circles so often assume they do. Faith is awe and mystery, questioning and wondering, room to breathe and room for the unknown. Faith is belief, even in the absence of certainty. That is true faith, true dependence on God.

Before I realized I was gay, I thought I had most of the

answers. Sure, I'd admit I didn't know everything, but I was pretty comfortable inside the box created for me and God to live in. Then I realized I was gay and suddenly nothing was certain. Propelled out of my comfort zone, the amount of uncertainty I faced was terrifying. *If I'm wrong about what God says on this issue, what else might I be wrong about?* I wondered. I felt as if my entire belief system might crumble beneath my feet. I was so frightened to step outside my box and look at things from a broader perspective, but when I did, each step made me realize just how small my box really was and how much I had confined God. Even by assigning only masculine pronouns to God, who is the creator of all and is beyond gender, I was limiting my understanding of who God is and can be in my life. Although adjusting to some of these paradigm shifts took time, I also reached the point where it felt insulting to put limits on the Divine, as I had done for so much of my life.

So I began to question. I began to wonder. I began to read, and I gained a broader perspective of history and culture based on contemporary research and archaeology. It was fascinating and eye-opening—and scary. One step at a time I began to deconstruct my theology and reconstruct it into what I believe to be a much more accurate understanding of God. I'm far from done, and the journey will probably continue for my entire life. But I'm so thankful for my church, which allows space for tough questions. It's led me to a place where I've become comfortable with not having all the answers—where I'm able to say, "I don't know," and feel at peace with that.

Coming out, stepping out into my true identity, and embracing myself for who God made me to be—*that* required faith. I knew coming out could have a price tag. I knew it would be questioned among my family and peers. I knew it could potentially cost me everything. But I wasn't prepared for the fact that it actually would.

Telling my family I was gay was the most nerve-wracking, difficult, and painful thing I've ever done. After confiding in my parents the most vulnerable personal information I could ever share with them, they stared at me with blank faces and told me they felt like I had died. Comparing my sexuality to murder, pedophilia, and bestiality, they took away my keys to the house, saying they no longer trusted me to have open access to their home. In the following weeks and months they continued to ostracize me from the family more and more, until I no longer felt safe to be with them and it was clear I no longer belonged. When I married my wife in 2014, I had no family present at my wedding, and several months later my parents cut ties completely. It was as if marrying a woman ended all hope they had of me changing my ways, and therefore they severed all remaining threads of our relationship. We haven't spoken since.

Losing my family, my relatives, many of my friends, the church I'd been part of for fourteen years, and the hometown I'd grown up in from the age of seven required faith unlike anything I'd ever known. I was completely and utterly dependent on God to survive, to pull me through, and to provide for me. Not having it all together, not having all the answers, not knowing what the future held, and yet taking each step forward as God asked it of me required more faith than anything I'd ever faced.

I've come to realize that we can know very few things with absolute certainty. Even science, which is seemingly foolproof, has been defied by medical mysteries. We must rely on faith—true faith that leads to complete dependence on the fact that God is loving and good and doesn't make mistakes.

A GOOD TREE CANNOT BEAR BAD FRUIT

In his Sermon on the Mount, Jesus says, "Every good tree bears good fruit, but a bad tree bears bad fruit. A good tree cannot bear bad fruit, and a bad tree cannot bear good fruit. Thus, by their fruit you will recognize them" (Matt. 7:17–18, 20 NIV). If you look at the life of a closeted LGBTQ individual, rarely will you see good fruit. Most of the time you will see suppressed emotions, internalized homophobia, fear, and an extreme desire to please and be accepted by God and others. Often you'll also see stems of self-hatred, depression, self-injury, and suicidal ideations, and at the very core, someone who does not believe they are worthy of love or belonging. Not one of those things is good fruit. All eat away at our hearts like a worm eats through an apple, damaging our physical bodies and killing our souls. Hear me loud and clear when I say: *That is not what Jesus wants for you.*

If you are still in a place where you believe that God somehow hates you for being LGBTQ, examine the fruit that keeping your identity hidden is producing in your life. What do you see? Is the fruit good? My guess is that the fruit you see is rotting and eating away at the core of your being.

Even as hard, painful, and challenging as coming out has been for me, I would never return to the life of certainty I once led, even though it was more comfortable. Faith may require discomfort and being stretched outside my box, but it has also led me to a much deeper, richer, and more fulfilling life. I am happier, freer, more at peace, more comfortable in my own skin, more complete, and more alive now than I ever was prior to coming out. I often say I feel like my life began the day I came out because I've never felt so grounded in joy and authenticity as I have since that day.

These are the good fruits that Christ talks about—the fruits that everyone should be experiencing. When you find the fruits of the Spirit—love, joy, peace, patience, kindness, goodness, faithfulness, gentleness, and self-control—regardless of whether people oppose you or not, you can rest assured that you are in the right place. Let those things abound in your life. As Galatians 5:23 says, "Against such things, there is no law" (NIV).

Being yourself and who you were destined to be can grant you freedom and joy in ways that right now you can only imagine. Yes, coming out has a cost; the road to authenticity rarely comes without a price. But the reward of coming alive and being unashamed of who you are is one of the most liberating experiences you will ever have.

If you're not sure what's going to happen when you come out, that's where faith comes in: when you get in the wheelbarrow. It's terrifying and freeing—all at the same time.

WHO DO I TELL FIRST, AND HOW DO I TELL THEM?

When you feel you are ready to start coming out, remember that you don't have to tell everyone all at once. Coming out may happen over a period of weeks, months, or even years. In some ways, we will always be coming out to new circles of friends, new jobs, and new people we meet. But as you begin to think about telling the people closest to you, use the following checklist as a guide.

Compile a list of everyone in your life
Write people down by name and categorize them according to groups: family, relatives, work colleagues, church friends, acquaintances, and so on. There will be people in all facets of your life to consider, but it will be more pertinent to some people than others when considering who to come out to about your LGBTQ identity.

Decide who you need to come out to and who you don't
Not everyone in your social sphere needs to be made aware of your LGBTQ identity. Those closest to you are most likely the ones who matter the most: your immediate family, your close friends, perhaps your boss or team at work. Often coming out in social or work circles is more for your convenience than their knowledge. The freedom of being out at work or in social circles grants you the ability to talk about your girlfriend or boyfriend, partner, or spouse without having to filter your pronouns in order to hide the truth. Being able to talk about the home project you and your wife just finished or the weekend trip you and your husband just returned from gives you a sense of belonging and normalcy in the

workplace and among your peers. Having to suppress who you are, even in these small ways, comes at a cost and eventually catches up to you emotionally, physically, mentally, and spiritually.

Still, telling every person you've ever met that you are LGBTQ would be unnecessary and exhausting. If it's not pertinent to your relationship with that person or you feel like your personal life is none of their business, scratch those people off your list. Instead, identify people you feel do need to know; the rest will either find out in time or will remain oblivious, which is completely okay.

Create a ranking order of people to come out to

Plan the order in which you want to come out to people. Start with someone you know is going to be supportive and happy for you. You want your first experience to be positive as it will boost your confidence for the next. Whether that person is a friend, family member, teacher, colleague, or mentor, identify someone you know is safe and gain experience by coming out to someone you trust.

Once you have your first positive experience behind you, start working your way through some of the acquaintances on your list. It will give you practice for the harder conversations and is less likely to greatly impact you if they aren't wildly supportive.

After you have some positive experiences and feel like you have a base of support, work your way further in to your inner circle. Maybe, like me, you tell a sibling before you tell your parents. Perhaps your mom is more accepting than your dad, or you prefer to start with your grandparents or a cousin. Slowly start working your way in, but be cognizant of telling people who know your family before you tell your family yourself. Even well-intentioned people can have a hard time holding onto a juicy piece of information. If your family finds out from someone other than you, they may feel betrayed and hurt that you didn't tell them first, which could further complicate your coming-out process.

Decide how you want to tell each person

You can come out to an individual or a group of people in any number of ways. The method may also be different with each person, depending on your comfort level.

Face-to-Face. It's hard to deny the power of stories, especially when they come from someone close to you. I've had several friends I knew prior to coming out who have told me that, because I came out and lived my truth, they completely reevaluated their position on LGBTQ inclusion. Those moments have been some of the most rewarding of all for me. On the flip side, I chose to come out to my parents and brother in person and at times have regretted that decision. Their reaction is forever burned into my mind. I've often wondered if writing a letter would have been a better choice. It wouldn't have changed their reaction, but it would have spared me the trauma of repeatedly reliving their initial shock. Ultimately, you have to do what you feel is right for you. Unfortunately, you won't really know if it was the right decision until it is over. At that point, regardless of the outcome, you'll have to make peace with the fact that you did what you felt was best in that moment and leave it at that.

Letter or Email. Some people choose to come out in an email or handwritten letter. This option is great if you are nervous about a person's reaction or have a hard time expressing yourself verbally. Writing gives you the chance to think through what you want to say ahead of time and be articulate about how you communicate. You have some control in making sure you are able to fully explain yourself and your journey before they interject. The negative aspect of written communication is that your intent may not always come through clearly, and sometimes words can be misunderstood. Still, writing is a useful and valid option for many people.

Video. Creating a video of yourself telling your journey to someone or a group of people is another option. It captures the personal element of seeing and hearing from the real you while guarding your heart against possible adverse reactions. To some, video is more personal than a letter or email and has less of a chance of miscommunicating tone or intent. If you tend to be verbally articulate but are afraid that questions or accusations may be thrown at you that you are not yet ready or equipped to confront, consider video, which is useful as well if you want to come out to someone "in person" who lives in a location you're unable to travel to in the near future.

Over the Phone, Skype, or FaceTime. A phone call is the middle ground between coming out to someone face-to-face and telling them in a letter or email. You're not there to physically see them while you communicate, which can be in your favor if you expect them to react poorly, but it still gives more of a human touch than is sometimes conveyed in a written communication. Skype and FaceTime are also options that provide a personal connection while maintaining some physical distance. If you choose one of these routes, make sure you set a specific time with the other person to talk. You don't want to catch them during an awkward moment when they are distracted by trying to get out the door for an appointment or put dinner on the table. Tell them you have something important you'd like to discuss with them and ask for a time where you'll have their undivided attention.

Social Media. Social media has the unique ability to communicate to large groups of people in a way that none of the above options can provide. I do not recommend that you come out to those closest to you via Facebook or Twitter. People in your inner circles deserve to hear it from you directly rather than at the same time you announce your LGBTQ identity to the virtual world. Social media, however, can be a helpful tool in conveying a message to a broader audience. Once you've come out to those closest to you, a social media post can explain where you're at to some of your extended friends and acquaintances without having to contact them individually.

Sometimes simply updating your relationship status or writing a post about where you are at in life not only gives others a frame of reference but also allows you to feel free to be yourself post pictures as you wish, and not have to the hide who you really are from the world.

Remember that there is no right or wrong way to come out. Decide what is most comfortable for you; no one else can do that for you. What is right for someone else may not be right for you. Trust your gut and do it for different people or groups in whatever way makes you feel most confident and secure. You are not responsible for other people's reactions to your truth, nor do you have the ability to control the outcome. The only thing within your power is making sure you do it at a time that is right and safe for you. Then make peace with the fact that, regardless of the outcome, you came out in the most respectful yet safest way possible for the circumstances.

WHAT DO I SAY?

Before moving forward in this chapter, please remember that I cannot predict every scenario you'll encounter or provide point-by-point answers that can guarantee for you a rejection-free or pain-free coming out. Instead, my goal is to give you issues to ponder, strategies to incorporate into your own situation, tools to equip you, and confidence that you can come out successfully and thrive regardless of the outcome.

There's no getting around the fact that figuring out what to say is difficult. This conversation is most likely one of the scariest you'll ever have. But as you formulate what you want to say, here are some guidelines to consider.

Think about the important highlights
Consider what you want this person or group to know about your journey of coming into your LGBTQ identity. Tell them what that process has been like for you.

Preempt some of their questions

Provide information such as how long you've known, when you first started realizing you were different, how this has impacted your relationship with God and others, and how this has affected you personally in negative and positive ways. Jot down some notes if that makes you more comfortable, and also so that you won't have to worry about forgetting what to say.

Talk less about theology and more about your heart's journey

Telling someone how this experience has uniquely affected you draws them away from the polarizing tendency to pit LGBTQ people against Christianity. If they can hear your heart, your struggle of accepting yourself, your breakthrough in affirming your identity, and the fear you face of being rejected by those you love the most, these issues will resonate with them and hopefully cause them to respond with more compassion and empathy, and less lecturing and Bible quoting.

If they ask about theology, point them to resources rather than engaging in a debate

Unless you are very confident in your ability to handle a theological debate, don't do it. Point people to resources where they can find that information for themselves. Those who really love you and want to learn will take the time to read and engage with the material. Those who are completely convinced that they are right will not budge from that belief no matter how much debating you do. Steer away from engaging with them and just continually point to where they can access that information for themselves.

You do not have to prove anything

You only have to speak your truth. For so long I felt like I had to prove to my family that I was still the same daughter they'd always known and loved. I didn't want anything to change. I wanted them to still be proud of me. In the end, all my efforts did nothing to make me equal in their eyes to the daughter they previously saw. It only disappointed and disheartened me. Release yourself from the "pressure of proving" and just be who you are. Speak your truth with boldness and without shame.

Only answer questions if you feel safe doing so

You need to be in a strong place to defend yourself against the questions that may come. If you're not ready for that, it is okay to say something along the lines of, "I'm sure you may have some questions, but for now I'd like just to share my heart with you. I'd appreciate if you give it some thought and take a few days to mull it over before asking any questions." If that person's reaction is positive and you feel safe to do so, open it up for any questions they might have. But if not, know it is okay to set that boundary of giving them some time and space to process before discussing it further.

Be confident

Some of the things people say may hurt or discourage you. Stand boldly in who you are. You've done nothing wrong by speaking your truth. Don't let them make you feel like you have. You don't have to change anything about your LGBTQ identity in order to be acceptable to God. You are beautiful and fully loved by God *exactly as you are*. Own that and ground yourself in it deep in your soul.

Have plans to do something afterward

You're likely to be wrapped up in a whole cyclone of emotions leading up to the day you come out. Have a plan of what you are going to do after the conversation is over. If you live alone, going back to your apartment and being by yourself all night is most likely not the safest plan of action. You need to be around people who affirm and embrace you for who you are. Make a plan to go out to dinner with some friends, go bowling with your buddies, or watch a movie with your best friend. You'll be glad you did.

I realize that not everyone has the chance to be methodical in how they choose to come out. Some people are outed before they are ready, some people are confronted before they want to be, and some people impulsively spew it out over Thanksgiving dinner simply because they can't stand being asked one more time if they are dating somebody without being able to answer truthfully. No formula is perfect, because people aren't perfect. We are human and we make mistakes, and life doesn't always fall into place in our preferred order. Use what you can to help you through your unique situation while realizing that no one but you knows what it's like to be in your shoes. Follow your heart with as much integrity as you can for both yourself and for others.

HELPFUL PHRASES TO USE AND THOSE YOU WANT TO AVOID

Helpful Phrases

LGBTQ. Use the appropriate acronym and the actual term (gay, bisexual, transgender, lesbian, gender nonconforming, etc.) to identify yourself and to reference the LGBTQ community. Modeling the correct terminology helps coach others how to do the same.

Sexual Orientation / Gender Identity. These terms are positive and scientifically accurate. Use them to describe the physical and romantic attraction of both LGBTQ and straight people, as well as the gender identity of both cisgender and transgender individuals.

Living Authentically. This phrase is great to use, especially in conservative circles, as it emphasizes living from a place of transparency and authenticity. The person you're talking with may not agree that God made you the way you are, but hopefully the other person *can* recognize your courage and vulnerability in sharing this piece of your heart with them in an authentic way.

Husband/Wife/Partner/Spouse/Girlfriend/Boyfriend. Name your significant other for what they are. Don't hide behind terms like "friend" or "roommate," and don't let others do that to you either. Calling an intimate partner a friend or roommate negates the significance and legitimacy of your relationship and is disrespectful to both of you. Don't be afraid to use terms like "married" or "wedding" if those words apply to your relationship.

Terms to Avoid

Same-Sex Attracted. This term is commonly used in conversion, reparative, or ex-gay therapy environments. They speak of same-sex attraction as a condition one "struggles with," but that can be healed or changed through therapy, prayer, and accountability. The majority of the time, if you hear this term used, the person has gone through ex-gay therapy themselves or is coming from a non-affirming environment that believes something about you needs to be cured for you to be acceptable to God.

Homosexual/Homosexuality. This word has come to be derogatory and triggering for many LGBTQ people. The term often comes up in a religious context to reference the clobber passages and condemn the LGBTQ community.

Queer. Be cautious with the term "queer." While many people from younger generations, mainly millennials to present day, are reclaiming the term "queer" and actually choosing to identify that way, those from Generation X and before (and sometimes even millennials like myself) can find this word triggering as it was commonly used in a derogatory sense or as a put-down to the gay community, especially gay men. Use this term cautiously and know your audience.

Transgendered. "Transgender" is an adjective, not a noun. Saying, "I know a transgender," "They are transgendered," or "We have to protect the transgenders" is incorrect. People are transgender. They are transgender females or transgender males, but they are not "transgendered," any more than a gay person is "gayed." It's an incorrect use of the term and demeaning to people who are part of the transgender community. The word "tranny" is also offensive, and "transvestite" and "crossdresser" are misused and outdated terms that do not describe people with a transgender identity. If we want to be respectful, we need to learn to use the terms correctly.

Lifestyle. "Lifestyle" is a very triggering word for LGBTQ people. It also arises frequently in religious circles to indicate that being LGBTQ is a sinful choice that needs to be changed, fixed, or healed.

Struggle. Many of us were taught growing up that we were supposed to fight against our earthly flesh or force our bodies into submission under the authority of God. As a result, our sexual orientation or gender identity was something we "struggled" with but from which we ultimately were supposed to be freed. This idea, whether used internally because of our upbringing or by others because of their religious beliefs, continues to be offensive as it implies that you need to be fixed or cured, rather than embraced and celebrated for who you are. "Struggle" is also commonly used in conjunction with "same-sex attraction" in the phrase "I'm struggling with same-sex attraction." Using "struggle," especially in the context of this particular phrase, only continues to imprint the idea that something is wrong with you that needs to be changed.

While this list is not exhaustive, all these terms can be used against you and make it seem like your LGBTQ identity is something sinful or a choice that needs to be fixed, cured, or healed. By choosing more affirming terms to identify yourself, you model your identity in a healthy way and avoid setting yourself up to be baited in conversation with others or mis-identified in a way that harms you.

WHAT IF MY FAMILY OR PARENTS ARE IN MINISTRY?

I hear this question often. Many of us who grew up in evan-gelical homes were taught to love and respect our parents and to honor them with our choices. We feel that by making our LGBTQ identity known, we are deviating from that core prin-ciple and derailing our entire family unit. The truth, however, is that you can't protect your family from everything forever, nor should you have to. Your parents are your parents, and as their child, it is not your job to protect them from the truth. Your only job is to live your truth. How they respond and what they do with that information is up to them. You can certainly come out in a way that respects them and their position and also allows you to be honest about who you are.

For me, with a father who has worked in such a prominent position at Focus on the Family for so many years, I knew that my coming out would have a large impact on our family. I remember telling my parents when I came out that they could tell or not tell whatever friends, coworkers, and so on that they wanted. I said, "I'm not going to flaunt it, but I'm not going to hide anymore either." Staying in the closet was suffocating my soul to the degree that I was well on my way to a death sentence. I couldn't hide who I was any longer, nor should I have been asked to—and neither should you. Many of you have fathers who are pastors or teachers at a Christian school, a mother who works at a prominent Christian nonprofit, or parents who are missionaries. If they are in ministry and as solid in their walk with God as they claim to be, they will find a way to walk this path, just as you have. Be gentle and respectful, but live your truth.

WHAT IF I'M IN MINISTRY?

Being in ministry yourself is a very different situation than if your parents are in ministry. If you are currently serving in a ministry role of any kind, you really have only two options. The first option is to be transparent in all aspects of your life. You tell your pastoral or ministry leader about your journey into your LGBTQ identity and risk the consequences of possibly losing your leadership position. The second option is to compartmentalize and decide to draw a hard line between your personal life and your professional life. My wife had to operate this way for many years as a gay person in the military under "Don't Ask, Don't Tell." By law she wasn't allowed to be openly gay until that policy was repealed under the Obama administration in 2011. For many years her professional and personal lives had to remain separate. Challenges come with compartmentalization as well, such as having to remain distant from your coworkers and being unable to share with your peers about your home life and day-to-day happenings. You probably won't have your partner or spouse accompany you to events such as holiday parties. So compartmentalizing comes with isolating factors and complications, but it can be done. You just have to decide what is right for you. Part of being a sexual minority means that you have the right to decide when you confide in others and how much. You make the choice as to when you want to share with someone about this very personal part of your life.

Choosing to separate your personal from your professional life now does not mean you will always have to be in the closet, and choosing to be transparent about your LGBTQ identity does not mean you will never be able to serve in ministry again. An increasing number of open and affirming ministries and churches are welcoming the gifts and talents of LGBTQ people. Ultimately, you need to protect yourself—whatever that looks like for you at this point in your life.

TO THE PARENT OR ALLY

Preparing to have this conversation with the people around them is one of the most terrifying experiences your LGBTQ loved one has ever had to face. Offer your support by lending a listening ear when they need to vent or process, or be a guinea pig when they need someone on whom they can practice their coming-out speech. Offer to listen to them read their coming-out letter to you before they send it, or take them out somewhere fun to get their mind off things after coming out to important people or groups. Also take note of the terms above and remember to use language that is inclusive rather than triggering for your loved one. Be in their corner in whatever ways you can to help them through a vulnerable time that feels very daunting and scary for them. They are going to need you.

6

Boundaries Are Not Disrespectful

Setting Healthy Boundaries

Daring to set boundaries is about having the courage to love ourselves even when we risk disappointing others.
—Brené Brown

Alex grew up in an affluent neighborhood of San Jose, California, and was raised in an Episcopalian church. His parents, who waited to have children until later in life, used the wisdom gained with age to model strict parenting with Alex while also fostering independence and free thinking. But when it came to religious beliefs, Alex's parents still leaned toward the conservative side of the spectrum. This was a bit ironic considering that the church they attended was quite progressive and consisted of a highly educated demographic that encouraged questioning one's beliefs rather than clinging to conservative theology. The parish taught that God could be found anywhere and didn't lie solely inside a church building, or even solely within Christianity. The church took youth group visits to mosques and synagogues as part of an interfaith study and cultivated an environment that led them to discover God for themselves. Alex felt fortunate that his parents somehow ended up attending and raising him in such a progressive church, even though both of them were religiously conservative.

His parents' beliefs became particularly important to Alex around the age of eighteen when he realized he was gay. Rather than have time to plan his coming out, Alex was found out by his parents. This new information immediately prompted his dad to tell Alex that he needed to draw closer to Jesus and pray to be cured. And although Alex was close to his mom in his childhood, in that moment when he needed that bond the most, his mom told Alex that he was dead to her. In an effort to fix Alex, they sent him to see the priest at their Episcopalian parish. Scared, vulnerable, and lacking the confidence to set boundaries with his parents with regard to his sexuality, Alex soon found himself sitting in the priest's office in anxious anticipation of what being found out might mean for his soul.

But entering the room with a smile, Father Norman instantly put Alex at ease. What followed deflated Alex's fear like a stuck balloon. Father Norman sat up in his chair and leaned in. Looking Alex dead in the eye and without hesitation he said, "Alex, God made you exactly the way that you are. There is nothing wrong with you—there is nothing that needs to be fixed. Your father is the one with the problem, and he's the one who needs to come see me." And that was that.

It was a defining moment in Alex's life. More than any other memory during that time frame, that moment imprinted itself on his heart. A burden was lifted from Alex's soul that day, and Father Norman's words shaped the way Alex viewed himself, LGBTQ culture, and religion as a whole moving forward. The priest's assurance granted him the courage he needed to proudly own his identity and set boundaries to protect it, without fear of what other people thought or of his soul being committed to hell. Had Father Norman's response been different, Alex might never have returned to church. But because Father Norman affirmed Alex's identity and place in the family of God, Alex continues to serve in that same parish thirty-seven years later. His relationship with God continues to evolve and deepen from that of his youth.

Although there were some rough years between Alex and his parents throughout college and in his twenties, and his parents ultimately moved away from that parish, Father Norman's words grounded Alex as he moved forward with his life. He no longer saw being gay and being involved in the church as a paradox. When he met Rob, who later became his husband, Alex wasn't afraid to love him. Alex felt resolute in his beliefs and stopped questioning why he felt the way he did. Instead, he embraced that part of his identity.

The continual support of Father Norman and others in church leadership empowered Alex to live out who he was meant to be. He married Rob in 2008, and they've served together in multiple church leadership roles there for many years. Before retiring, Father Norman even encouraged Alex to run for the vestry, saying, "If you want the next young person who is questioning who God made them to be to hear the same affirmation that you did, you need to be involved to ensure the right priest is hired." Alex joined the vestry, and the new priest they brought on is the one who married Rob and him.

Support and affirmation from those in spiritual leadership roles granted Alex the confidence he needed to affirm his own identity and stand strong in that, which is why chapter 3 of this book is dedicated to finding an affirming and hopefully spiritual community. For Alex, it also played a vital role when it came to dealing with his in-laws, who believed both Rob and Alex were going to hell. Because Alex knew who he was and who God created him to be, he didn't crumble under the weight of their projected beliefs. He was able to stand strong and tell them that he wouldn't waver in what he believed. Instead, if they had questions, he told them that he was happy to set up a meeting with his bishop or parish priest. Setting a boundary like that is something he most likely wouldn't have been able to do without the certainty that his priest instilled in him during his teen years. That defining moment gave him the assurance he needed to carry him for a lifetime.

Establishing and maintaining boundaries is hard. Not many people enjoy talking about the subject, but boundaries are essential to the health of humanity, and they are so much easier to establish if you are confident in who you are and what you believe. If you're still dealing with your own internalized homophobia and aren't convinced that God really loves you or that you even belong in the family of God, setting boundaries that protect your beliefs will be hard. You have to resolve your internalized homophobia and restore your sense of value and worth before you can be effective at setting boundaries.

Boundaries are also much easier to set if you have a community affirming your identity. Even in moments when you waver or are unsure, you have people holding you up and standing beside you. Some people are strong enough to plant their feet against the current on their own, but others are not. Know yourself—what you can handle on your own and where you need support—and honor that.

The topic of boundaries is especially tough if you come from a conservative or evangelical background. Many of us were taught that voicing an opinion that differed from our parents was disrespectful. "Children should be seen and not heard" may not have been verbalized, but it was embedded in the family ground rules. Even more so, "Honor your father and mother" kept us submissive and silent. Rather than honoring the discussion that comes with varying viewpoints, they were seen as a threat to the values and structure of the Christian family. We were expected to do what we were told and to obey the first time—without questioning.

When I first came out and began setting boundaries with my parents, in many ways for the first time, it completely threw them for a loop. They didn't know what to do because they had never seen me establish the rules. I had always been the easygoing, people-pleasing daughter who followed the rules and did what she was told. When I broke that paradigm and told them I was going to spend part of my holiday with friends before coming to see them, or that I no longer felt comfortable discussing my sexuality with them in a private setting, my parents couldn't even process this new reality.

"Is someone feeding you these lines, Amber? Because we know you and this is not you," they'd say with such assurance. I'm not sure if they were trying to convince me or themselves, but they certainly didn't like that at the age of twenty-seven, I was no longer doing as I was told.

The truth is that I *was* seeking counsel from others during that time because boundaries were just as uncomfortable and new to me as they were to my parents. It was just as challenging for me to set and enforce boundaries as it was for them to accept them. But two things I knew for sure: first, after their response to my coming out, I no longer felt safe around my parents. Being compared to murderers and pedophiles and having my house key revoked did not create an emotionally safe space for me to have civil discussion and disagreement with them. Second, after a lifetime of suffocating isolation, I did not want to have to wear a mask to make other people comfortable ever again. It was sucking the life from my soul. To me, coming out wasn't going to be worth it if I was only going to be sort of alive and halfway free. I needed to allow myself to be completely free, even if that meant sacrificing the relationships I'd held most dear.

In the end, I did lose those relationships. But in hindsight years later, I wouldn't want them back if it meant having to live bound to perfection and chained to silence again. I wouldn't change my decision to come out, because it's what allowed me to finally be who God created me to be. It's absolutely the best thing I've ever done. But setting boundaries was a crucial step toward freedom and one that I believe is important for everybody, regardless of their experience or background.

Boundaries are not disrespectful. They are healthy, they protect our hearts, and they set us free. As author Doreen Virtue says, "Boundaries are a part of self-care. They are healthy, normal, and necessary."

THE COMPLEXITIES OF A SIMPLE YES AND NO

What boundary-setting means for you and how it plays out in your life will be unique to your situation. If you work for a Christian organization, you may have to set boundaries for yourself about how much you share with others in order to prevent discrimination. If you work in the private sector and have colleagues who are insensitive to who you are or who you love, you may need to set verbal boundaries with them as to what they can and cannot say around you. Maybe that means stopping a joke that demeans the LGBTQ community or correcting them when they use hurtful terminology. Whatever your workplace's boundaries look like now, begin mentally preparing yourself in advance to reset them where necessary.

Some of you will need to set boundaries with friends who now think you're a bad influence simply because they're aware of your LGBTQ identity. Perhaps you'll have to set boundaries at church in order to either protect yourself from further hurt and rejection or to protect your leadership position (depending on how you decide to handle church in conjunction with your LGBTQ identity). But the majority of us will, to some degree, need to set boundaries with family members: parents, siblings, grandparents, in-laws, or extended family. And setting boundaries with family is one of the hardest things to do.

Take a moment, though, to think ahead with me, for a few months or a few years. Imagine a future for yourself in which you've chosen not to set boundaries. Perhaps it starts with your grandpa introducing your girlfriend or boyfriend to others as simply your friend, and you let it slide. Next, you overlook the fact that your significant other isn't allowed to join you at home for the holidays. You think to yourself, *That's okay. We'll each spend time with our respective families this year and then celebrate together when we both get home.* Or if you're transgender, you reluctantly accept but don't press the fact that your father refuses to call you by your chosen name and use the pronouns that align with your innate gender identity. Perhaps you dismiss the fact that your mom discounts your relationship by not including your spouse in family photos. You may agree to sleep in separate beds or even rooms while under your parents' roof in order to spend time with them. After all, you don't want to cause a ruckus; it's just for a few nights.

Over time, one compromise turns into another and then

another. Soon, turning a blind eye to this behavior is just what you do. You do it because it makes it easier to be in relationship with your family. But easier for whom? It certainly makes your family comfortable; they are getting what they want—a relationship with you without having to acknowledge this piece of your identity that forces them to reevaluate their beliefs, ideas, or stereotypes. Soon, and possibly without even realizing it, you've lost your self-respect because you've allowed yourself to be consistently degraded and dehumanized. Years have passed, and while you've still been able to spend time with family, it hasn't been quality time. You've felt suppressed and dismembered, rather than alive.

Though we don't like to call it such, these types of behaviors are passive-aggressive and either directly or indirectly communicate blatant disrespect for your gender identity or sexual orientation by minimizing who you are or the significance of who you love. By subjecting yourself to that kind of treatment, over time you begin to believe that is all you are worth. Boundaries are very hard to establish. You have to believe that you are worthy of love and belonging in order to feel confident in establishing healthy boundaries.

WHERE AND HOW DO I START?

No matter where you are in your journey, *it is never too late to start setting healthy boundaries.* Yes, if you have allowed your family to get by with demeaning your LGBTQ identity in order to keep the peace, you will most likely come up against some frustration and questioning when you start incorporating healthy boundaries into your life. However, neglecting to set boundaries in the past does not keep you from setting boundaries now.

Remember that the person you are setting the boundary with doesn't have to understand why you are setting a particular boundary; you may or may not feel safe telling them the reason. However, they do have to respect it. But in order for other people to respect you and your boundaries, you have to respect yourself enough to set and maintain them.

So where and how do you start setting boundaries? You start setting them in the place that is causing you the most turmoil or pain, and you start setting them now.

WHAT IS A HEALTHY BOUNDARY?

Recognize where someone else ends and you begin
Someone else may hold the belief that being LGBTQ is of the devil, is damning your soul to hell, and is responsible for the current calamities in our world. Just because they hold that belief does not mean that you have to, and just because they believe something is the gospel truth does not make it so. You can choose to set a mental boundary that separates you from them and decide not to absorb or take on that belief, regardless of how much people try to convince you that they are right. You have a right to believe truths that cause you to feel whole and healthy. Sometimes boundaries come in the form of cognitive, intentional decisions to separate from people or beliefs that are toxic to you.

Clearly communicate to someone what is and is not okay with you
Your friends may feel that their job is to tell all your other classmates about your recent coming out, or your sibling may feel the need to proselytize and project their beliefs onto you, but you have the responsibility and the right to tell them that it is not okay for them to tell other people about your LGBTQ identity, or that you do not want to have a conversation around religious beliefs about this topic. Telling people about your LGBTQ identity is an intimate event, something that only you should hold the right to do when and if you feel safe. Likewise, having a conversation about religious beliefs is very personal ground that you should only walk with those who are willing to really listen. Though these are just two examples

of an endless list of possible scenarios, know that a big part of healthy boundaries is clearly communicating to someone what is and is not acceptable to you.

Respect someone's "no" and don't pressure them to change it

In the words of Anne Lamott, "'No' is a complete sentence." You are not required to justify your reasoning or give an exhaustive commentary to everyone about the inner workings of your heart. You have the right to set a boundary and have it respected. Likewise, your family has the right to set their own boundaries as well. Unfortunately, because this topic is so heated and sensitive, sometimes those boundaries will come into conflict. Sometimes your nos will be in complete opposition and bring you to a standstill. However, if you want them to respect your no, you also need to respect theirs.

Respect yourself enough to stand your ground

Setting healthy boundaries comes from being rooted in respect: for yourself, your significant other, and your loved ones. You don't want to waste people's time by allowing your boundary lines to vacillate, nor do you want to bring more harm to the situation by saying one thing and then doing another. Communicating clearly and standing firm in what you believe and the boundaries you set will foster respect in your relationships and help you respect yourself even more.

PRACTICAL EXAMPLES OF BOUNDARY-SETTING

Boundaries and Conversations about the Bible

People often ask me whether they should debate Scripture with a family member, friend, or pastor. Most of the time, my answer is no. I've found that people who hold deep-seated beliefs around the literal interpretation of the Bible and same-sex relationships usually have no genuine interest in trying to hear or understand you. They know what they believe and only want to engage in a discussion to prove why they are right. Therefore, no matter what you say or how good your argument is, they are never going to move or change their views. It is wasted energy for you, not to mention emotionally exhausting and taxing.

People who truly are curious about what it means to be both LGBTQ and Christian will take the time necessary to read a book and educate themselves. My website has a list of books for people who genuinely want to grow in their understanding of the Scriptures around this topic. Let those folks do the work themselves. Just as it is not the responsibility of people of color to educate white people about racism, it is not the responsibility of LGBTQ people to educate straight people about homophobia, transphobia, or misinterpretations of Scripture. Yes, you can have healthy dialogue and answer questions as you feel comfortable, but don't make it your job or mission to change the mind of every person you meet on their beliefs around LGBTQ inclusion in the church. A handful of people feel called to do that, and thank God for them. But for most of us, it is unnecessary and even traumatizing to repeatedly try to justify to others why we deserve to exist in the world. Let those who are disingenuous take their argument elsewhere.

Boundaries and Social Media

Social media is one of the best and worst inventions of our day. It can connect us with long-lost friends and pit us against one another in the worst ways. It can unite communities in crisis and tear families apart. It can make you feel loved in hard times and feel greater isolation than you've ever known. As a culture, we have a love/hate relationship with social media.

For LGBTQ people, connecting via social media can help you feel less isolated than previous generations who had very limited ways of searching out affirming ministries or supportive groups. But it can also be the tool used to ostracize us from our families and friends when posts pop up on our wall showing pictures of birthdays we should have been a part of celebrating, family reunions we should have been invited to attend, and memories of nostalgic holidays from years past.

Removing my family from my Facebook account so that I could no longer see their posts was one of the hardest boundaries I had to set. By that time, communication with my family had dwindled to almost nothing, and Facebook was the only window I felt that I still had into their lives. But it was also the ghost that haunted me as I watched my family take vacations without me, my dad continue to struggle with his health without anyone letting me know, and my mom bond with my sister-in-law and adopt her as a surrogate replacement of the daughter she shunned. But as hard as it was, it was the healthiest thing I could do for myself. It was a boundary I needed to set for my own well-being.

I removed some other friends over time, and some I've kept even though we don't speak. None of them were removed out of hate or kept due to a hidden agenda. It was a matter of doing what I needed to do to keep myself healthy and safe. I also didn't make all the changes overnight. It took time, waves of courage, and the ability to grieve those lost relationships. But the personal Facebook friends I have now are people who affirm me and with whom I feel safe. I purposefully keep my personal Facebook community small and intentional so that I have a place to be myself and share the inner workings of my life with those closest to me, separate from who I am as a public figure. For me, it is important to have that safe space.

Evaluate your social media interactions. Maybe you need to delete some friends to make space in your mental feed for new ones. Consider unfollowing, unfriending, or blocking people who bring toxicity instead of life to your soul. Don't get caught up in the ugly, spiteful hatred that can be the social media world. But do take care of yourself and do what your heart needs. There's no reason to feel guilty about setting boundaries in place.

Boundaries and Communication

When and how you talk to people about your LGBTQ identity is a decision that only you should make and is based on how safe you feel. You don't ever have to stay in a conversation where you feel threatened or exposed past the point of comfort, which includes conversations with parents as well as people in leadership. I know that is contrary to what we've been taught, and setting a boundary that prematurely ends a conversation is a scary thing to do, but you need to remember that you have agency—that is, the capacity to act independently and make your own free choices. You are not trapped. It is perfectly healthy for you to state in a calm manner that you are no longer comfortable continuing the conversation at this time and choose to walk away. Phrases like, "I'm not ready to have this conversation with you," or "I'd be willing to continue this conversation once you're in a calmer state of mind," are also very acceptable. What you want to avoid is escalating into a shouting match or becoming frozen because you feel trapped to the point that you can no longer engage in healthy conversation. Setting a verbal boundary early on will help you prevent those situations from happening.

With that said, feeling uncomfortable and feeling unsafe are different. You will have conversations with people in which you feel uncomfortable. But if you feel like the person you are talking to is genuinely trying to understand, I encourage you to push through the discomfort. You never know what good might come from having that conversation; the person may end up becoming one of your biggest allies. However, if you are feeling unsafe or like you're being degraded and backed into a corner, that is very different from feeling uncomfortable. Any time you feel put on the defensive, it is absolutely healthy and right for you to stop the conversation.

If you've set a verbal boundary but the other person in the conversation is unable to respect it, you may need to consider other forms of communication. I eventually became so uncomfortable around my family that I had to resort to emails and letters as opposed to verbal and face-to-face communication.

Another option is to bring in an unbiased third party, such as a licensed family therapist, to help bridge the divide. I encourage you not to use a pastor, church therapist, or layperson because they often come with biases about family structure and LGBTQ people. You need someone who can help you and your family come to a place of mutual respect and understanding, without trying to sway anyone's theology or beliefs one way or the other. Having these tools in your resource pack and knowing about them before you need them will be helpful when you are struggling to feel heard and valued.

Boundaries and the Holidays

I think holidays are one of the most painful times for LGBTQ people regardless of whether they have contact with their family or not. Unless you are one of the fortunate few whose family completely embraces you with 100 percent affirmation, holidays are probably challenging and stressful for you. Whether you feel excluded because of your LGBTQ identity or you feel like an outsider looking in, whether you feel less than human or like you have to hide who you are in order to spend time with your family—all of these are painful ways to spend a time that is meant for celebration and connection. Holidays are among the most difficult and the most important places to set healthy boundaries.

So many people I've spoken with want me simply to give an answer and say what to do, but I can't do that. I can only give you tools to equip you to do what you feel is right, when you feel ready to do it. That may mean you decide not to go home if your significant other can't accompany you and be treated with mutual kindness and respect. It may mean you decide not to go unless they honor your relationship as equal to everyone else's. It may mean that you decide you'll go only if they use proper pronouns and call you by your chosen name. It may mean that you and your significant other agree to separate for a day and visit your respective families and then celebrate together later. It may mean that just the two of you celebrate, or that you only have a meal with your family rather than stay for the whole holiday, or that you only go every other year, or that you only call home rather than visiting. There are many different options and ways to spend your holiday time. Do what is healthiest for you—even if it is not the easiest.

Sometimes both parties are happy with the outcome; sometimes they aren't. It is wonderful when you are able to work out a situation where both you and your family are happy with how the holidays play out, but unfortunately that is not always the case. Sometimes neither person ends up getting what they really want. In my situation, my parents wanted me home for the holidays, but not my wife. I wanted to be able to bring my wife home with me and be treated as equal to my brother and his wife. My dad told me, "Amber, you are always welcome in our home, but Clara will never be welcome under our roof. That is something that will never change." I chose to set a boundary by saying, "Dad, if Clara isn't welcome in your home, then that means that I am not welcome in your home. She is an extension of me. You would never go somewhere for the holidays where Mom wasn't welcome and leave her alone for the holidays. You can't expect me to do that either." Because in that area neither of us was willing to compromise, the unfortunate result was that we never spent another holiday together. But neither of us won that argument. Neither of us got what we really wanted: to spend holidays together as a family.

Boundary-setting isn't about who wins and who loses. It's about self-worth, self-respect, and how you are being treated as an LGBTQ individual inside your family. Sometimes protecting your significant other and the love you share means losing someone else or something that you really love and care about. I still encourage you to do it. You're worth it.

TELL THEM HOW IT MAKES YOU FEEL

One of the most powerful tactics for disarming an argument or passive-aggressive behavior is to call attention to it in a calm and respectful manner and tell them how that behavior makes you *feel*. Your family member may not always see the harm their dismissive behavior is doing to you, so telling them how their words or actions affect you personally can often—though not always—make them rethink the way they are acting. When engaging with them in this way, make sure you use "I" statements as opposed to "you" statements. Making "you" remarks or accusations such as, "You didn't invite me to Mother's Day brunch," or "You refuse to call me by my chosen name," instantly puts people on the defensive and causes them to feel under attack. Instead, change your comments into "I" statements: "I was hurt that I wasn't included in the Mother's Day brunch. It made me feel ostracized from the family," or "It is painful for me when the fact that I'm transgender isn't acknowledged. When I'm not called by my chosen name, it makes me feel like the core of who I am is being erased."

If your family is planning a reunion and invites you but not your significant other, you could say something like, "I understand that it makes you feel uncomfortable to see us together, but by not including [name of your partner] in this gathering, it makes me feel [dismissed, unloved, angry, forgotten, cast out] because I am not able to enjoy making memories with them as a family the way my [brothers, sisters, cousins] and their spouses are able to."

People can argue about their own behaviors and intentions, but they cannot argue how it makes you feel. These basic communication skills can be applied to any relationship but are especially helpful when trying to establish an understanding around how a person's behavior influences another or why boundaries are necessary. You can begin practicing this skill in all areas of your life. The more you become aware of how a situation makes you feel, the easier it will be to stay calm and communicate that feeling to others.

WHEN TO HOLD ON
AND WHEN TO LET GO

A question people often ask me is "When do I engage [or reengage] the conversation of inclusion with my family, and when do I let it go?" In other words, when do I push through the pain, and when do I cut ties or a take a step back from the relationship? First of all, just like no one can tell you when it is time for you to come out, no one can tell you when it is time to engage or cut relationship ties either; only you can do that. The matter is too delicate for a blanket answer.

People can encourage you to be brave and push through—or see the harm it is causing you to stay and encourage you to take a step back—but in the end only you know when it is time and only you will have to deal with the consequences, good or bad. The primary question I tell people to ask themselves is, *Do I feel safe?* Safety in these conversations is vital because they touch on such deeply personal and vulnerable parts of our hearts and lives. If you do not feel safe—physically, emotionally, mentally, or spiritually—then I encourage you to step back from the relationship and put some boundaries in place. They may only be temporary, but keeping yourself safe and healthy is always priority number one. You do not have to tough it out, and you *never* have to keep yourself in a dangerous or toxic space.

If you do feel safe to engage or reengage the conversation, then do so. Do it slowly and with caution, especially if you are reentering waters that have previously produced some waves, but slowly wade back in and see what happens. If it doesn't go well, step back and establish a boundary before proceeding. If it does go well, take another step, and then another. Trust your gut. Set boundaries as needed, and acknowledge how you are feeling throughout the process. That way, no matter what happens, your integrity and your self-respect will remain intact.

QUESTIONS TO PONDER
REGARDING BOUNDARIES

In the end, only you can decide what you are and are not willing to handle and when you are ready to set boundaries. As you move forward, ask yourself these questions:

— How much stress am I putting myself under by allowing [fill in the blank]?
— Is it worth it?
— What is one area of my life in which I would like to see better boundaries?
— What would those boundaries look like?
— How will this boundary help me feel more healthy and whole?

Routinely taking an inventory of your internal measure of safety and how you are feeling in different areas of your life will serve as a compass moving forward to help you navigate what paths to walk down and when. If you become intimidated or afraid, talk about it with a trusted friend and see what they think about the boundary you're trying to set. Sometimes just having validation can give you the strength you need to see it through.

TO THE PARENT OR ALLY

Boundaries are a difficult topic and make just about everyone uncomfortable to some degree. The important thing is to encourage and respect healthy boundaries in all areas of life. That goes for both you and your LGBTQ loved one. I also encourage you to call your loved one by the pronouns or terms by which they prefer to be called, as a gesture of respect. This respect should also extend to transgender people in regard to calling them by their chosen name. Deadnaming—the act of calling a transgender person by their birth name rather than their chosen name—whether intentional or unintentional, does not honor the person they are or their journey. Calling them by their chosen name acknowledges that you see them for who they truly are and extends respect to them as a human being.

If you're unsure of the pronouns or terms someone prefers, ask! Most LGBTQ people would rather have questions asked than assumptions made. When people assume, they risk labeling their LGBTQ loved one incorrectly or unintentionally using a term that is uncomfortable to them. I personally prefer the term "gay" rather than "lesbian" when referring to my identity, but people wouldn't know that unless they asked me. Technically "lesbian" is not incorrect when referring to my sexual orientation, but I am more comfortable with "gay," and many other women feel the same way.

Asking someone, "What gender pronouns do you prefer?" or "How do you identify?" is perfectly fine. Starting the conversation also then opens it up for further curious questions and opportunities to learn. Your loved one will appreciate the effort you are making to understand them better and label them correctly. It's not intrusive; it's helpful, and we appreciate your willingness to learn and grow in your understanding of the LGBTQ community.

7

Am I Worth It?

The Value of Tending to Your Soul

Food for the body is not enough. There must be food for the soul.

—Dorothy Day

In 2007 I embarked on an adventure to climb Pikes Peak with my friend Stacy. Pikes Peak is the beautiful fourteener (a hiker's term for a mountain between 14,000 and 14,999 feet high in elevation) along the Colorado Springs Rocky Mountain range. It is also the mountain where "America the Beautiful" was penned. With thirteen and a half miles and an increase of nearly 8,000 feet in elevation between you (and your pack) and the top of the mountain, hiking Pikes Peak is not for the faint of heart. Stacy and I trained all summer for this day and now it was finally here. We pulled our cars into the trailhead parking lot at 4:30 a.m. and began our venture in the dark, intending to follow the hiker's rule that says to be off the mountaintop by noon in order to avoid storms that can quickly roll in after 12:00 p.m. I outwardly acted brave as we started our sun-deprived trek up the mountain, but secretly I was using my flashlight to check the bushes for wild creatures. Just about anything could be out looking for their morning meal at 4:30 a.m.

As the sun came up and the hours passed, the mileage between us and the top of the mountain slowly dwindled with each step of our hiking boots. Unfortunately, we hadn't even hit the halfway mark before the hip flexor muscle I'd torn earlier in the season started to ache. The way it was feeling told me it was going to be a long trek up the rest of the mountain. But being the deeply determined person that I am, I pressed on, depending on my hiking stick for support and resolute in my decision to make it to the top. Despite my best efforts, the ache in my leg inevitably slowed us down, therefore denying us the ability to reach the peak by noon. Before we knew it, the clouds rolled in quickly, as they often do, and we were caught above tree line without shelter when it began to storm. Finding momentary protection under a rock to break out our ponchos, we knew waiting it out wasn't our best option. We were already wet and tired, and the air was thin. Hypothermia wasn't an unrealistic prospect. We knew the best thing to do was to press on.

Reaching the final ascent before arriving at the top, we came to what they call the Sixteen Golden Stairs. But let me tell you: the experience is anything but golden. What they don't tell you ahead of time is that those "stairs" are actually sixteen switchbacks that you must conquer at the very end of your trek in order to reach the summit—when you're exhausted and gasping for air, and your legs are shaking. Tired, wet, and now cold, we pushed on one awful step at a time until we made it through each of those sixteen hellish stairs.

I had envisioned arriving at the top to be a glorious moment, full of feelings like accomplishment, achievement, success, and mountaintop bliss. But in reality, it was quite anticlimactic as we arrived at the top only to realize that the last train of the day, which we certainly wanted to be on, was soon departing down the mountain. We snapped a picture, bought a T-shirt to prove we'd completed our mission, emptied our bladders in an actual bathroom, and hopped on the train that would take us toward home. Arriving at the bottom, we did feel accomplished, but we also felt the effects of our accomplishment—tired, worn down, and a little beat-up. Craving comfort and relaxation, we both headed to our respective homes for a hot bath, some dark chocolate, and a glass of wine. It was quite the adventure, and neither of us regrets it—in fact, we still talk about it fondly to this day—but in those hours between starting off in the darkness before dawn and summiting the mountaintop, we sure had some fearful moments, some exhausting moments, and some moments where we just plain wanted to give up.

Coming out can feel a lot like hiking a fourteener. Just like Stacy and I trained on numerous mountain trails before attempting the big summit, preparing to come out may feel like preparing for a difficult climb. You read books like this one and others as a map to help you navigate the trail ahead. You practice coming out on some easier trails (people who you know will be affirming) before braving the big summit of telling your family. You gather all of your coming-out gear and equipment—your affirming community, a good therapist, and healthy boundaries—making sure they are all in your pack before the big day. You do everything you can possibly think of to prepare yourself—and then you set out in the dark wilderness to brave the unknown.

Like me with my flashlight in the dark, you may outwardly act brave, but inwardly you're terrified of what you might face. *What am I going to encounter at the next turn? What might this cost me? Will I make it to the top? Will it be worth it?* These questions rattle round and round in your head, but with each step forward you are more determined than ever to face your fears and make it to the summit.

Inevitably, no matter how much you prepare, you will encounter some unexpected bumps on the trail and face some inclement weather that slows you down. It's just a fact. You can't foresee everything that is to come. But when you reach that point of wanting to give up, don't stop. *Press on.* Listen to that voice deep inside you that says, "You're almost there. You can do this. You will make it." Keep your eye on the summit: the freedom that comes with being fully alive and wholly, authentically you. It is worth the climb.

Reaching the top of coming out may not feel climactic. It may not be the big moment you were hoping for, where you shout from the mountain's peak, "Here I am! This is me!" and feel instant relief pour out from your spirit that you've finally arrived while everyone throws a celebration in your honor. Yes, you may feel relief upon coming out. All the anxiety you've harbored for months or years is finally released because, regardless of the outcome, you've said it out loud and spoken your truth. But just because you've reached the mountaintop doesn't mean you've done so unscathed. You could feel like you've finally arrived *and* like you're beaten up, tired, and weary. They come hand in hand. And once it's over and you've reached your "coming-out summit," it's important to take some time for self-care and focus on tending to your soul after the climb.

Perhaps you're feeling the pain that comes from the loss of a relationship or the hurtful words of a family member. Perhaps you've been let go from your position in ministry at church or you've been rejected by someone very dear to you. Perhaps you're in a mixed-orientation marriage and being authentic means parting ways with your current spouse so that you can both find the joy and happiness that you deserve while figuring out how to tend to your children's needs. All these painful and difficult situations leave bruises and wounds that we carry forward with us—and they take time to heal. Just like my bubble bath, dark chocolate, and wine at the end of my climb, self-care for your heart is warranted and needed. You've earned it, your soul is important, and you need to listen to what your heart tells you it needs. Respect yourself enough to lean in to these methods of self-care and find value in these areas to help your heart heal and be whole.

HAVING A HOBBY AND TRYING NEW THINGS

Anytime we go through a big transition in life, we need an outlet for our stress. It may be different things for different seasons of your life, but coming out is a great time to try something new. Maybe you've always wanted to try salsa dancing or pottery or woodworking. Explore those options. Various forms of art and music are wonderful ways to express yourself. Maybe you release stress by painting on a blank canvas or through songwriting or poetry. Maybe you join a book club or find a hiking buddy. I am a big proponent of getting outdoors and letting nature whisk you away from the busyness and stress of life. Yoga, meditation, contemplative prayer, or an early morning walk on the beach are all fantastic ways to start your day with a clean slate and flush the cortisol (or stress hormones) out of your body. Whatever appeals to you, whatever breathes life to your soul—do that. If you're not sure what breathes life into you, take time to try several new things. You might find that some are particularly good at relieving stress while others help you process your emotions and others still are just plain fun. Be gentle and gracious with yourself. Do what your heart needs.

CONSISTENCY

In challenging times it is often easy to feel like everything is spinning out of control and you have no anchor. In those moments it is helpful to have some consistency in your schedule and something on which you can depend. Establishing a routine, even in simple ways, can help ground you when so many things feel beyond your control. Having steady work hours and a set schedule can help. Knowing that you have dance class on Mondays or book group on Thursday nights gives you something to look forward to each week. Maybe you take your dog for a walk each evening or have coffee with a certain friend every Saturday morning. Be intentional in scheduling your down time. Isolation can abound if you have too much time on your hands and nothing to fill your calendar. Grounding yourself with even a few consistent, steady, ongoing items on your schedule can help immensely with your stability.

WATER AND A BALANCED DIET

This may seem like common sense, but a balanced diet is often one of the first things to go when we become stressed. Instead we eat more, don't eat at all, or turn to junk food for comfort. But what our bodies really need, especially during stressful times, is clean, healthy foods. Protein, fruits, nuts, and vegetables provide our body with the energy and nutrients it needs to function and help our brain think more clearly during times where stress is clouding our judgment. Drinking plenty of water is also a kind thing to do for yourself as it helps flush out all the toxins your body is holding on to during stressful periods. I'm all for the occasional frozen yogurt or chocolate bar; comfort food is called that for a reason. But as a whole, be intentional about what you put into your body during this time so that you can think more clearly and make better decisions when confronting stress.

PET THERAPY AND COMPANIONSHIP

As I mentioned in chapter 3, it wasn't until Half Pint, my Shih Tzu–Maltese mix, entered my life in 2009 that I realized the immense power of having a pet. I'd never bonded with an animal growing up and therefore never really saw the benefit of having a dog in my life. But after adopting Half Pint at ten weeks old and bringing her home, I was in love forever.

Studies now show that having an animal can reduce blood pressure and playing with or petting an animal can increase the stress-reducing hormone oxytocin and decrease production of the stress hormone cortisol. Not only that, but pets also help reduce our level of loneliness and isolation. Knowing that there is someone that is always happy to see you and who greets you with enthusiasm every time you walk through the door becomes a great comfort when you're struggling with rejection and loss. Pets also help with consistency. Simply knowing that someone relies on you for simple things like food and water helps you establish a routine. Dogs in particular also give you a reason to go for a daily walk or two.

Beyond the physical benefits of having a dog or cat, the emotional benefits are also quite powerful. When given the proper love and care, this pet can become your new best friend. Dogs are loyal. They lend a listening ear when you feel you have no one left, they are there to cuddle and love you every time you need them, and they stay in your life even when people don't. Dogs don't see gender or orientation. They only see love. And the love and care you give to them comes back to you countless times over in laughter, cuddles, and companionship. If you're not at a place in your life where you have the time or financial means to properly care for an animal, find other ways to get some pet therapy. Volunteer at an animal shelter, try some goat yoga (I swear, it's a thing!), enroll in equine therapy, or offer to pet-sit for your friends when they need it. Whatever you can do to work in time with some furry friends, make that a priority. I almost guarantee it will make you feel better.

FORGIVENESS

Ever since I was a teen, I've loved the story of *Tuesdays with Morrie*. Something about soaking up wisdom from a person further along in life than you is like rich food for my soul. If you haven't read the book or seen the movie, *Tuesdays with Morrie* is the sweet story of a professor who is dying of amyotrophic lateral sclerosis (ALS; Lou Gehrig's disease) and decides to give his final thesis on life in his last few months. Bringing everything he's experienced and learned to the table, he talks about the importance of living, knowing how to die, love, and forgiveness. He had many aphorisms, or as he liked to call them, "sound bites for the soul." One of my favorite sound bites involved the concept of forgiveness.

Morrie tells the story of a quarrel he had with a dear friend earlier in his life that, due to their own stubbornness, severed their relationship and caused them to lose touch. Years later, Morrie learned that the man had died of cancer. They'd never had the chance to reconcile their friendship, and Morrie missed out on telling this man what he really meant to him. Regret washed over Morrie, causing him to evaluate himself and lean into the importance of forgiveness. Laying in his bed with the paralysis of ALS working its way up his body and into his lungs, Morrie says with strained breath to his buddy Mitch, "Forgive everyone everything. *Now. Don't wait.*"

"Forgive everyone everything." I can almost hear you thinking, *Easier said than done*, and I'd agree with you. But I think we often misunderstand the meaning of forgiveness. Our culture has painted forgiveness as weakness, conveying the message that to let go of someone's wrongdoing against us is the equivalent of losing or giving up our power in the situation. But it is actually the opposite. The more we hold on to unforgiveness, the more bitterness, anger, and resentment take root in our soul. Forgiveness isn't an act of weakness that lets the other person off the hook; forgiveness is an act of power that sets our own soul free from a life of entrapment to them. Nadia Bolz-Weber does a great job of reframing the conversation by saying, "Forgiveness is about being a freedom fighter."[1] And who doesn't want to feel more freedom in their soul? Forgiveness isn't easy, but it also doesn't have to be complicated. It is the act of refusing to hold on to something that ties you to a person in a negative way. Forgiveness isn't saying what they did to you is okay; forgiveness is acknowledging that what they did is wrong but that you will not be held captive by it. It's taking back your power, not giving it up. So, yes, forgive everyone everything—because that is how you keep your heart clean, light, and free.

LETTING GO

Sometimes the harder life gets, the more we tighten our grasp on the people and places we fear losing the most. We pull our relationships, friendships, and leadership positions in closer and closer to our hearts. We may even find ourselves thinking, *If I lose [blank], I don't know what I'll do. I don't know who I am without that.* But the tighter we grab hold of something and the more we try to control it, the less authentic it becomes. It's unnecessary and unhealthy for you to stay in a position out of fear or to keep someone in community with you because you don't know how to live without that person. That is not authentic living.

As scary as it is, sometimes the best thing we can do is to loosen our grip on that which we fear losing the most and let things happen as they may. You don't want to stay somewhere that is toxic for your soul. That harms your emotional as well as your physical health. Many people develop significant health issues as a result of harboring their true identity and staying in an unhealthy environment. We have to let people have the freedom to be or not be in our lives. Otherwise it is not genuine community. By loosening the death grip you have on those people and things most precious to you, you then have the opportunity to see which ones are real and which are not. Yes, it is hurtful when some of those people decide to walk away. But it also opens our eyes to see who really has our back and where we really are safe and where we are not. By letting go of the unhealthy places in our lives, we create space for new and more affirming opportunities to fill those holes. The transition between the two can be painful, but the end result is rewarding and full of life.

STARTING NEW TRADITIONS AND ESTABLISHING A NEW NORMAL

One of the hardest things about coming out and not being accepted by those around you is finding your new normal. Where once holidays with your family were a given and vacation time or college break was automatically assumed to be spent back home, you now have a lot of new adjustments to make. Going home may now mean tension and awkward conversations, or it may no longer be an option at all. Holidays may pose difficult decisions about who you will spend time with, where, and for how long. These changes feel like a jolt to the normal you previously enjoyed and perhaps even took for granted, serving as a continual reminder that what once was, no longer is. That's hard and painful, and it means facing a huge adjustment.

Moving forward, you are going to need to find or create a new normal, and the exciting part is that you get to determine what that looks like. The difficult part is that it may not feel the way it used to or include everyone you want.

Since coming out, holidays have been one of my biggest challenges and most painful reminders of loss. My mom did holidays well, going out of her way to make them special and meaningful. For that to suddenly disappear from my life was devastating. Not only did I not get to share in making those memories with my family, I also didn't get the privilege of bringing my wife home to share in them. As a result, we've had to work on creating a new normal when it comes to the holidays, and honestly we've had different degrees of success. Some holidays have brought enough joy to fill that empty space, and at others I just wanted to completely fall apart. Sometimes they happen in tandem.

We've taken some intentional steps toward fostering and welcoming a new normal in our lives. For me that has meant carrying on some of the traditions of my youth, like the fall celebration we call the Great Pumpkin Dinner. My wife and I still enjoy hosting a new group of friends for that autumn feast every year. But we've also created some new traditions that are entirely our own. My wife is Filipino and enjoys making sushi, so we've started the tradition of making California rolls as an appetizer before our meal each Thanksgiving. We've also often done what we call an Orphan Easter where we open our home to anyone in our church who doesn't have somewhere to go for the holiday. We've made some dear friends that way, and it is our way of breaking apart loneliness and bringing people together in community.

Experiment with some new traditions of your own. You might surprise yourself with the things you find or enjoy. It may not always be smooth and perfect, and that is okay. Allow space to feel and grieve whatever you need to in those moments when the pain of loss comes. But also work on creating a new normal that you can live with and that brings joy perhaps not only to you but also to others.

TIME

In this age of microwaves, high-speed internet, drive-thru food joints, and two-hour home grocery delivery services, culture feeds our desire for instant gratification. But not all things are best when they're instant, and not all wounds heal with a swab of alcohol and a Band-Aid. You need to make friends with time. Time teaches you and guides you along your journey. Time can heal your wounds, creating distance and space between your pain and your current reality. Time lends you perspective. But time will not grant you immediate gratification, nor should we want it to. In the moment, it's easy to want to fast-forward through our suffering. We want to rush past our pain and say we've come out on the other side. But if we speed through time and the experiences that come with it, we deny ourselves the opportunity to grow, learn, expand our understanding, and strengthen the very core of who we are. Accept where you are, breathe deeply often, and let time teach you as you sit in the midst of where you are, in your life, at this moment.

LETTING YOUR LIFE BE YOUR EXAMPLE

Now that you are out, people will likely be watching you. Some people you will never reach with your words, and others you need distance from in order to keep yourself healthy and emotionally safe. But certain others will be quietly watching from the sidelines. They may not say much, but they are observing from a distance your life and the way you live. You get the opportunity to show them a piece of what the diverse family of God can look like. It may happen over a period of months or even years, but you never know whose life may be drastically influenced by your example. Your bravery in being authentic just might be the catalyst that changes someone's views on LGBTQ inclusion in the church and moves them to a place of full acceptance of LGBTQ Christians.

If you're reached the mountaintop of coming out, be proud of yourself. You did a very brave and courageous thing. Take a deep breath and soak in the beauty and pride of being true to who you are. If, like me, you're feeling a little beat-up and bruised, know that it is normal to need some time to recover after reaching a milestone this large. Be gentle with yourself, give yourself some grace, and incorporate the values discussed in this chapter in order to tend to your soul. You are worth it.

TO THE PARENT OR ALLY

If your loved one has recently come out, chances are they are feeling the pain that comes from being rejected by those who don't see their true worth or place in the family of God. As their parent or ally, it is your job now to help foster that. Help them cultivate some of these new values in their life, support them by celebrating their LGBTQ identity and the boldness it took for them to come out, and continue to communicate that you love them just the way they are. Whether they admit it to you or not, they need to hear those words from you right now—and they need to hear them often. They will second-guess themselves and their decision to come out every time they are met with hesitation or rejection. Affirmation from you will help grow their confidence in those moments. Support them in trying new things, offer to go with them as they look for a new hobby, and help them be creative in finding traditions to create their new normal. They will want and need to lean on you during this time, but they may not want you to know or see how much. So be there for them, love on them, and support them in whatever ways you can during this critical time of transition.

8

"I Love You, but . . ."

Coping with Conditional Love

Love is the absence of judgment.
—Dalai Lama XIV

"I love you, *but* I don't support your marriage."

"I love you, *but* agreeing to disagree is the same as condoning your behavior, and that is something I will never do."

"I love you and want to know about your friends, *but* we need you to know that we do not condone same-sex relationships."

"I love you, *but* don't you want kids? If you transition, you will no longer be able to have children."

"I love you, *but* if I came to your wedding I would have to answer to God for supporting your marriage."

"I love you, *but* this is against what the Bible teaches, and I have to stay true to the Bible."

"I love you, *but* I won't be involved in your homosexual lifestyle."

"I love you and you will always be welcome in our home, *but* if you ever get married, your spouse will never be allowed under our roof. That will never change."

"I love you and I love your children, *but* you know that supporting your LGBTQ child is a sin."

"I love you, *but* divorcing dad to marry a woman was wrong. I forgive you, *but* I'm not ready to talk or have a close relationship like we used to have."

"I love you and want to be a part of your life, *but* I can't because you are living in sin. I will never let anything come between me and God."

"I love you, *but* I don't condone your chosen lifestyle. You obviously have not looked at what God says in Scripture."

"I love you, *but* God does not want me to have LGBTQ friends."

Each of these are actual statements that LGBTQ people have heard from family, parents, children, pastors, and lifelong friends. When asked how these words made them feel, people reported a wide range of emotions: frustrated, belittled, betrayed, undermined, manipulated, and hurt were just some of the responses.

One person admitted that they knew they were gay at a very young age but knowing that their parents' love was conditional and that they believed being gay was a sin, that person suppressed how they felt, wrestled in isolation, and turned to watching porn to try and cure themselves in order to be acceptable to their family and to God.

Another person divorced her husband after realizing she was gay and her children completely cut her out of their lives. Her son graduated college and even got married without ever contacting her to let her know. In a recent letter, he said he loved her and forgave her, but still didn't want to see her or have any part in her life.

Still another person said they felt that their entire relationship with their parents and family hung under a cloud of, "I love you, *but* . . . ," unable to ever be truly seen, heard, or understood.

As LGBTQ people, these statements leave all of us with a strong, dull ache in our hearts—and rightly so. Following "I love you" with the word "but" inserts a condition that must be met in order to be loved and accepted. It diminishes our worth and makes us question our ability to belong.

In this chapter I explore the damage that conditional love has on us as LGBTQ people and discuss how to heal our hearts from that pain in order to develop a healthy spiritual life. The section for parents and allies of LGBTQ people is longer in this chapter, as we talk about the harm that statements such as, "I love you, but . . . ," and other triggering phrases have on LGBTQ people's hearts and lives.

GRAPPLING WITH LOVE THAT FEELS LIKE LIP SERVICE

Almost every LGBTQ person has heard an "I love you, but . . ." statement. However, if you were raised in a conservative evangelical home or another conservative religion, the chances are that you heard those statements more often and also heard them paired with a comment about your inability to have a relationship with God, and even to have an acceptable afterlife, unless you changed. These statements damage our self-worth and destroy our souls. It's manipulation masquerading as love. It's unacceptance cloaked in acceptance. It's love with strings attached. Ultimately, the person using the statement might as well be saying, "I will only love you *if* . . ." However they fill in the blank, the person wants you to repent and turn back to God: that is, they want you to be straight and cisgender.

I remember my mom saying, "The door is always open, Amber, if you ever want to come back to Jesus and come back to us." She couldn't bring herself to understand that I'd never left. I was still the same person she'd known before I told her, only I had to grow a lot of courage and strength at record speed to keep up with the way my family treated me now that they knew I was gay. But she could no longer see *me*; she could only see my sexual orientation. I'm sure a million questions struck fear in the pit of her stomach in the weeks following my coming out. But instead of deciding to grow courage and strength alongside me, she felt like she had to make a decision between her relationship with her daughter and her relationship with God. She told me to my face that she would choose her relationship with God over me, so the unconditional love I'd been told as a child that both God and my parents had for me proved to be untrue. Their love came with strings attached because they saw God's love as coming with strings attached. When tested under fire, those strings singed and severed. Every "I love you" from that day forward was followed by a "but," and whatever followed the "but" was all that I heard.

Countless LGBTQ Christians have experienced this exact same story with their own loved ones. It's scarring, representing love in its most superficial state. In order to process the pain that comes in those moments, we need to recognize that lip-service love is often rooted in fear: fear of the unknown and fear of what they don't understand. The act of recognizing and naming fear doesn't take away the pain that stings our hearts when we feel like we've been loved with a caveat, nor does it condone superficial love, but recognizing and naming fear does help us open the window of compassion on our hearts to see that people don't know what they don't know. And perhaps just simply knowing *that* will enable us to give them a little grace.

I'll be the first to admit that it is not easy. You'll need to dig deep in your tool kit and utilize the strategies we've talked about thus far in order to help you through. Tools like your affirming community (who express "I love you" statements that end with a period instead of a comma), your boundaries (verbal and physical, which we discuss more later in this chapter), and a good therapist (to help you process and let go of the pain that these caveats of love create in our hearts). At this point, you should be practicing and implementing the tools we've talked about so far. Don't be afraid to step out and start utilizing them. Your heart is worth the effort and your soul is worth the fight.

HOW TO AVOID PROJECTING ONTO GOD REJECTION FROM YOUR FAMILY AND FRIENDS

Feeling that God has rejected you is hard. I want to honor that and explain that I understand how difficult it is to separate the hateful and hurtful things being done and said to you in the name of God from who God actually is. When we've been brought up in an environment that speaks on topics with unquestionable authority as if they are speaking for God, it is easy to see a spokesperson—a parent, pastor, and so on—as the indestructible and infallible voice of God. When we hear that we are going to hell for being gay or bi or trans, we believe them. When they say we can no longer serve in ministry, we accept it, and when they insist that we no longer belong in the family of God, we think they must be right. We buy into the lie that we have to change something or fix a part of us in order to be acceptable to God. But that is bad theology—absolutely untrue and steeped in harmful, works-based beliefs. With God there is no "but" after "I love you." There is one simple concept that Jesus teaches over and over, and it is soaked in unconditional acceptance: love.

You must learn to separate what people say and do in the name of God from who God actually is. If you don't know much about who God actually is, start a journey of discovery. Find the truth about your place in the family of God and remind yourself of it often. The tools below can help you let go of the bad and make room for the good to sweep in and captivate your soul.

CULTIVATING A HEALTHY SPIRITUAL LIFE

When you've been hurt and rejected by people in the name of God and religion, it is easy to distance yourself from the Divine and even from spirituality altogether. Reclaiming that connection is a slow and often painful process, but it is so rewarding when you can do it in a way that feels both safe and inspirational to you. Here are some things to consider as you move forward in cultivating a healthy spiritual life.

Give yourself permission to look outside the box

If you've had your theology fed to you your whole life and were never allowed to think for yourself or to question what you have been taught, chances are you've put God in a pretty small box. Without the ability to question, doubt, and wonder, you will never expand your view of God or your understanding of the Divine. You have to be willing to break open that box and allow space for the unknown in order to discover the wonderful mystery that comes with a God that is much bigger than the God you thought you knew. Release yourself from fear and allow your view of God to evolve over time. We do not serve a stagnant God. We serve a God that is brilliant and full of hidden mysteries that we get to uncover—a God that is all-knowing and can teach us to know; a God that created life in forms as spectacular as cells, photosynthesis, and adaptive species; and a God that also created mysteries and wonders as great as the Milky Way, volcanic lightning, and solar eclipses. Our God is huge, with creativity wildly beyond our imagination. We put God in a box because it makes us comfortable, but putting God in a box is an insult to the Divine's creativity and diversity. We need to be courageous enough to set ourselves free from enslavement to comfort and come to know just a sliver of how vast and magnificent our God really is.

Examine your beliefs

If you've grown up in any conservative religious environment, take some time to examine whether what you believe is actually found in the study of Scripture or if the belief is merely a teaching of the church leaders. Sexual ethics (for example, the wave of purity culture) immediately comes to mind as an example of one concept that the church has, in my opinion, done a very poor job of teaching. There are many areas to be examined and ways to develop a healthy skepticism around what you were taught in your childhood. Beginning to look at Scripture through lenses of historical and cultural context can enhance your understanding a great deal. Even if you become frustrated in the process of deconstructing some of your beliefs, as is perfectly natural, in the end it is still worth the cost in order to reconstruct your faith into a healthier and more accurate understanding of Scripture and of God.

Redefine your view of God

Perhaps your view of God is so distorted that you have to develop an entirely new outlook altogether. Maybe you can no longer work within your current view of God. Perhaps you were taught to see God as an angry father, a punisher, or one who sits in the sky just waiting to strike you with lightning if you do something wrong. If that is the case, you need to completely nullify and bury that God and allow yourself to find God anew in imagery and ways that feel safe and comfortable to you. I love *The Shack* for this very reason. Portraying God as a middle-aged black woman completely defies the image of God that most people erect in their minds. It gives your brain a bit of a jolt, causes you to evaluate your stereotypes, and remember the fact that God is actually neither male nor female. Those binaries are labels we assign to make the image of God more comfortable to us. Later on in the story, the author changes images and presents God to Mack, the main character, in the form of an elderly Native American man. The point is that God will come to us in whatever form we need God to come, in order to meet us where we are.

Find God in unexpected places

You don't have to be in church in order to find God. God is everywhere all the time. God can be found in nature, in a song on the radio, in the smile of a stranger, or in the love of a puppy. God can be found in a text from a friend, in the wind when it blows on your face, or in the hug your child gives you before going to bed. Richard Rohr says, "We cannot attain the presence of God because we're already totally in the presence of God. What's absent is awareness." Heighten your awareness; make space for short moments in your day to take inventory of where you've seen or experienced God's presence. Write them down in a journal if that helps, or put them on little notes into a blessing jar. Whatever it is, make space for your soul to be still and raise its awareness of a God who is all around you.

Surround yourself with people who reflect Christ

It's helpful when cultivating a healthy spiritual life to surround yourself with people who are doing the same: asking hard questions and digging deeply into what it means to be a modern-day follower of Jesus. Look for people who are critically examining the Scriptures and who are not afraid to fight for all of those who are oppressed. They should not only be affirming of LGBTQ people, but they should also be equally concerned about the Black Lives Matter movement, about immigrant children being separated from their parents at the border, about human trafficking, about equal access to health care, about our Muslim brothers and sisters, and about the homeless, the disabled, and the underprivileged. They should be actively fighting for equality for all people—*because that is what Jesus would have done.* Surround yourself with these kind of people and not only will you learn and grow in your spiritual walk, but together we can make a more just and loving world for everyone.

HOW THEN DO WE PRAY?

Praying for those who have harmed us is difficult, especially those who do it repeatedly or intentionally. It's also hard to justify the prayer that says, "God, change their hearts. Bring them to an affirming place," when you know they are praying the exact prayer in reverse by saying, "God, change their hearts. Help them come back to you." It seems a moot point—like the two somehow cancel each other out. Does that then mean that we just don't pray for them at all? What if, instead of praying that those people change, we shift the position of our hearts and pray for God's best for them? What if we pray for things like joy, peace, health, and providence to be abundant in their lives?

In all honesty, I struggle with it myself. I don't want harm to come to the people who have hurt me, but I don't often feel like praying *for* them either. It's still a very raw and painful place. If that is where you are, God understands the intentions of your heart and sees the wounds you carry.

But if you're in a place where you do want some guidance on how to pray, let me offer some counsel from the words of Jesus in his Sermon on the Mount. He said, "You're familiar with the old written law, 'Love your friend,' and its unwritten companion, 'Hate your enemy.' I'm challenging that. I'm telling you to love your enemies. Let them bring out the best in you, not the worst. When someone gives you a hard time, respond with the energies of prayer, for then you are working out of your true selves, your God-created selves" (Matt. 5:43–45 *MSG*). Living out of our God-created selves is where all of us should strive to be. It's a healthy, beautiful place where bitterness and resentment cannot survive, and where life flows in abundance.

I think it also serves us well to pray for ourselves. Pray for the healing of your own soul, pray for bitterness and resentment not to take root in your life, pray for the ability to forgive and maintain a clean heart, and pray to love well. By staying in tune and keeping your own heart in check, it helps you take the focus off the actions of others and concentrate on your own wholeness and happiness. It doesn't take away all the pain, but it does keep your spirit in check.

TERMS AND PHRASES TO AVOID

In the process of writing this book, I surveyed a group of fifteen hundred LGBTQ Christians and asked what some of the most hurtful terms and phrases were that had been personally used against them because of their LGBTQ identity. I felt it important to include them in this chapter both for the LGBTQ person (to name the terms that have been spoken over us as a community and validate the pain that accompanies it), and also for the loved ones of LGBTQ people who may be using some of these phrases without even realizing they are harmful.

Terms to Avoid

Alternative lifestyle

Choice

Dyke/fag/faggot

Gay agenda

Gender-confused

Homosexual/Homosexuality

Lifestyle

Queer *(depending on the person/audience)*

Same-sex attraction

Sexual brokenness

Sexual preference

Tranny/transvestite/cross-dresser

Transgenderism/transgendered/transgenders

Phrases to Avoid

"Struggling with same-sex attraction."

"Your identity is in Christ, not in your homosexuality."

"Love the sinner, hate the sin."

"It's okay, we are all sinners."

"I love you, but I know this is not God's best for you."

"God will not/cannot bless that type of relationship."

"I have lived longer than you have, and I know this will not end well for you."

"You will not inherit the kingdom of God."

"I'm afraid your soul is in jeopardy."

"You're going to hell."

"Your life is going to be very hard because of the lifestyle you chose over God."

"I know the reason you are [LGBTQ] is because [fill in the blank]."

"It's just a phase."

"Why would you choose this over your own family?"

"All sin is equal in the eyes of God."

"I'm afraid this might rub off on my child."

"Being around you is a bad influence on me / my family / my kids."

"How selfish of you to do what makes you happy and not think about how this impacts us."

"I feel like you've died / you are dead to me."

To the LGBTQ Person

I know that these words and phrases sting and hit a very sensitive, painful place in your heart. Each of them makes my heart ache as well. And I am sorry that any of you have ever had to hear words that make you feel like you don't belong, or you don't measure up, or you'll never be good enough to be accepted into your biological family or into the family of God. It's not okay. And I want you to hear that.

I also want you to hear some important things about the people who use these words. These terms and phrases are most commonly heard when one or both of the following are in place: either the person using them lacks the education to realize the insensitivity of their words, or they are using these words intentionally to hurt or manipulate the result they want from you by fueling fear and discomfort. You can usually tell the difference between the two by observing the person's body language and tone of voice. Those who are simply ignorant aren't intentionally trying to hurt you and are generally open to having a conversation to learn about why those terms are hurtful. Those who are being manipulative will become defensive when confronted and always have an answer ready to justify their behavior.

What we must remember is that people who use these terms in order to intimidate aren't worth giving our time to in the first place. And those who use these terms to concoct a certain result (usually to change you or alter your behavior into a version of you that makes them more comfortable) are operating out of a place of fear themselves. They have invested so much of their lives in a belief system founded on fear that they don't know how to operate outside of that. They're afraid of losing you to hell; they're afraid of endangering their own souls to hell; they're afraid of what other people will think; they're afraid of losing their reputation, their job, their leadership position, or their relationships—or all of the above. They're even afraid of God. They're simply afraid.

That by no means condones their use of any of the words

or phrases listed above. Dehumanizing another person is never okay, no matter what the basis is. But it does help us understand them a bit more and develop empathy for the state of fear in which they live. Just like you feared being rejected by those you love when you came out, your loved ones have a coming-out process of their own. No, it is not the same as being LGBTQ, but if they affirm you, it is possible that they may pay some of the same consequences.

However, any time these words or phrases are used against you, regardless of who is using them, you have the right to set boundaries. I encourage you to start with a verbal boundary that brings attention to the word or phrase they've used and explains why that particular term is hurtful or offensive. Remember to practice "I" statements as we discussed and talk about how the word or phrase makes you feel. Identify the emotion you're feeling and own it. Don't be ashamed of it. An example would be, "Mom, it really hurts me when you refer to my bisexuality as a choice. By saying it is something I choose, it belittles what I'm going through and makes me feel like I am not equal in your eyes." Or, "Grandpa, I noticed you used the term 'homosexual' when referring to LGBTQ people. I thought it would be helpful for you to know that term is actually outdated now and is triggering for many people in the LGBTQ community. When I hear that term, it causes me to feel shame about who I am rather than proud. I personally prefer the term 'gay' and would appreciate it if you used that word to identify me moving forward." Simply calling attention to a term that harms you can make the person using the term more aware of how that directly affects you and makes you feel.

If a verbal boundary is not effective, you may need to take it a step further and implement a physical boundary, perhaps by distancing yourself from them until they are able to treat you with mutual respect. It is important to not lose sight of the fact that you are a human being, just like they are, and you deserve the same amount of dignity and consideration that is given to everyone else. Who you are is nothing to be ashamed of.

TO THE PARENT OR ALLY

Reflect on whether you've ever used one of these phrases or terms to describe your loved one's gender identity or sexual orientation. If so, how do you think that made them feel? How would it make you feel if someone said that to you about who you love or how you self-identify? How would having these things said to you impact your relationship with that person? Would you still feel safe to open up to them? These are questions I encourage you to ponder if you genuinely want to improve your connection with your LGBTQ loved one.

You may have said some of these things because you are afraid, and perhaps you didn't know you were being hurtful. Maybe you thought tough love was the answer, or maybe you just didn't know what to say. We've all done things out of fear or ignorance, and we've all made mistakes. The best thing you can do to have a healthy relationship with your LGBTQ loved one is to own your mistake. Rather than ignoring it or brushing it aside, be brave and find a way to communicate to your loved one that you are sorry for hurting them in this way. You can say something simple like, "I'm really sorry for telling you that being gay is a choice. I understand now how hurtful that must have been for you to hear," or "I'm sorry for calling you gender-confused. I'm trying to learn more about what it means to be transgender, and I really want to understand what you're going through." Expressions of genuine remorse can go a long ways in healing your relationship. It doesn't make everything instantly okay; trust is rebuilt slowly over time. But it is a good place to start. If you're not able to communicate this to them verbally or face-to-face because of the boundaries they've set in place, consider a heartfelt card or letter to express your remorse to them. Be patient with them. It takes time to rebuild trust when you've been hurt so deeply for something over which you have no control. But keep trying. Don't give up.

Another way to improve your relationship and communication is to talk with your loved one about some of these terms and phrases. I did not annotate each of them and explain why they are hurtful because I want you to have the opportunity to engage with those around you whom these words have wounded. If you're unsure why one of these terms or phrases is harmful and you're truly interested in learning, find a good time to bring it up to your LGBTQ loved one and ask them how that word or phrase makes them feel, and why it is damaging to them. If you do it with a sincere and humble heart, you have the opportunity to open the door for meaningful conversation to take place. Approaching it without your own agenda and a genuine desire to learn is critical to the conversation. If you approach it from a place of openness, it can help heal your relationship and grant you the ability to have a greater understanding of what life is like in their shoes.

It is important to remember that what you sometimes think is loving actually makes your LGBTQ loved one feel patronized and misunderstood. Statements like, "I love you, but . . . ," never communicate love. All the LGBTQ person hears is that they are unacceptable and unlovable as they are. It makes them feel invisible and like they can never measure up. Therefore, it often results in anger, pain, and distancing from those they love the most because of the pain that's incurred. Be intentional in using positive, affirming words of love when communicating with your LGBTQ loved one—love with no strings attached.

9

If Your Heart Is Aching

Restoring What's Been Lost

Have patience with everything unresolved in your heart and to try to love the questions themselves as if they were locked rooms. Don't search for the answers, which could not be given to you now, because you would not be able to live them. And the point is to live everything. Live the questions now. Perhaps then, someday far in the future, you will gradually, without even noticing it, live your way into the answer.
—Rainer Maria Rilke, from *Letters to a Young Poet*

If you're still with me at this point in the book, my hope is that you've learned a lot of valuable tools and are feeling much more equipped for your coming-out journey. Implementing these ideas and principles into your own story can help you thrive as you move forward. But I know that regardless of how full your tool kit is, I can't do or say anything to erase the pain of the rejection or discrimination you've faced simply for being who you are. You're going to feel a range of emotions, and you need to allow yourself to feel them. Suppressing how you feel so that no one, including yourself, can see these emotions is not going to help move you forward. You have to be brave enough to allow yourself to engage with the pain when it comes. Just a few of the types of loss you might be grieving after coming out are:

— Loss of relationships you held dear
— Loss of acceptance
— Loss of privileges or rights
— Loss of leadership positions at church
— Loss of family time around holidays

— Loss of safety
— Loss of dignity, value, or worth
— Loss through being disowned or abandoned
— Loss through being ostracized or manipulated by passive-aggressive behavior
— Loss through ghosting or distancing from loved ones or friends

Each of these valid types of losses can affect us profoundly. We need to give our heart the care it requires to be able to work through the pain associated with each of these losses. This is where incorporating the tools that we've discussed in previous chapters—like getting out in nature, expressing yourself through art, having a good friend you can rely on, or finding a good therapist—becomes key to navigating your way through the healing process. Some other helpful ideas are to write in a journal or perhaps write a letter—that you won't send—to one of the people with whom you're struggling to be in relationship.

Maybe you just need to sit and have a really good cry. That is totally normal and okay. Give yourself space for that.

Choose the tools that work best for you to help move you forward through healing; what works for your friend may not work for you. Find what does work for you and do it consistently. Each tool can help you engage with your emotions in a healthy way so that they don't bottle up inside you. Coming from someone who's been the master of bottling emotions, let me tell you, you don't want to take that path. Bottling emotions is toxic and only leads to additional heartache. Without a healthy way to process your pain, you inevitably will find an unhealthy way to process your pain: alcohol, food, shopping, self-harm, sex, overexercising, drugs, or whatever your vice is will emerge to numb the inner turmoil you feel. And working your way back to health from that place is much harder than if you just found the courage to face your pain to begin with. Yes, it's difficult, especially for those of us who have had our trust repeatedly broken by others or have had our feelings minimized when we've voiced them in the past. But facing the pain head-on is the better way.

I'm still working on it myself, and I probably will be for the rest of my life. Voicing my deep emotions does not come naturally for me. Only since coming out and meeting my wife have I begun to learn what it means to talk about and process emotions in a healthy manner. Talking about how you feel comes easier for some people, but we can all work on it. Richard Rohr says, "When happiness eludes us—as eventually, it always will—we have before us the invitation to examine our programmed responses and to exercise our power to choose again."[1] Coming out is your opportunity to examine your programmed responses and learn how to grow from them.

Most people are aware of the five stages of grief: denial, anger, bargaining, depression, and acceptance. But often as LGBTQ people we are fooled into believing that we are the only ones who think or feel the way that we do, and so we struggle in isolation. Below are some examples of what these five stages look like specifically for the LGBTQ person, and also for the parent of an LGBTQ child who has come out. My hope is that by sharing these with you, you will realize that you are far less alone than you feel, and that working through these five stages of grief is normal, and is a healthy part of your healing process.[2]

KÜBLER-ROSS'S FIVE STAGES OF GRIEF ADAPTED FOR LGBTQ PEOPLE AND THEIR FAMILIES

Denial

Denial is the first stage of grief, when the information we've received or our realization that we are LGBTQ is a shock to our system, and we enter survival mode. We go numb, refuse to accept the facts, and cling to an alternate reality that we long to be true. For us as LGBTQ people, that alternate reality is to be straight or cisgender or both.

Statements LGBTQ people might say or feel when in denial

— "I just haven't found the right person yet."
— "I just need to get out and date more."
— "This isn't the way I'm supposed to be."
— "Maybe it's just because I haven't had sex."
— "If I ignore it, it will go away."
— "I just need to try harder to be straight/cisgender."
— "I just need to fast and pray more."

Statements parents of LGBTQ people might say when in denial

— "It's just a phase."
— "I don't want to talk about this with you."
— "You just haven't found the right person yet."
— "I know you, and this isn't who you really are."
— "I don't want to hear about your LGBTQ life or the person you're dating."
— "This happens to other families, but not to mine."

How to move through denial

As you open yourself up to questions about your LGBTQ identity and the grief you are experiencing, you begin to allow yourself to move through the healing process. The feelings of denial begin to fade as reality comes to the surface. Permitting yourself to look honestly at this reality will bring many of the emotions you've been denying to the forefront, but it will also help you move through your denial and further into your process of healing.

Anger

Anger is a necessary and important part of our grieving process. It is also the emotion that surfaces when we begin to come to grips with our new reality or LGBTQ identity. We become upset with ourselves and others, looking for someone to lash out at or blame.

Statements LGBTQ people might say or feel when in anger

— "Why was I even born in the first place if this is how I was going to be?" "I hate myself and I hate God for making me this way."
— "God, why aren't you answering my prayer for healing?"
— "What did I do to deserve this?"

Statements parents of LGBTQ people might say when in anger

— "How could you shame our family like this?"
— "This is so selfish of you. How could you do this to us?"
— "I'm disappointed in you."
— "We were good parents! This is not our fault!"

How to move through anger

Anger is powerful and, at times, overwhelming. But the more you can open up to truly feel your anger, the more it will begin to dissipate, allowing you to move toward a place of healing and wholeness.

Bargaining

Bargaining is that point in our process when we try to escape our current reality by promising to change or reform a part of our lives. We negotiate and plead with God to "fix" us (i.e., make us straight or cisgender) and promise any myriad of things in return, including prayer and fasting, a life of devotion to ministry, or a life of celibacy. Guilt is bargaining's companion and reveals itself, especially for parents of LGBTQ people, through the "What ifs?" and "If onlys" that rampage our minds as we replay the past in search of answers to the present and new reality.

Statements LGBTQ people might say or feel when bargaining

— "I will dedicate my life to ministry, God, if you just take this away and make me straight/cisgender."
— "If you don't fix me, I will walk away from faith all together."
— "I'll pray and fast as much as you want, God, as long as you cure me."

Statements parents of LGBTQ people might say when bargaining

— "You can be gay, but you can't act on it."
— "What you do on your own is your life, but I don't want to hear about it, and I don't want you to bring anyone home to meet us."
— "You may think you're transgender, but you can't act that way around us."
— "If you want to stay in contact with us, you'll keep this to yourself."
— "I'll help you get into ex-gay therapy where they can cure you of this."

How to move through bargaining

In bargaining we try to manipulate our new reality in order to avoid facing it. While this is normal, sitting with your new reality, regardless of how uncomfortable it may feel, will help you move forward into health and acceptance.

Depression

Many of us know about depression all too well. Especially as LGBTQ Christians, we feel the weight of depression hover over us for an identity we can't control. Depression is the stage where we resign ourselves to the truth of our new reality and sadness and despair set in. Fog may cloud our brain and we withdraw from life activities we normally enjoy. We also may experience fear or uncertainty about our future.

Statements LGBTQ people might say or feel when depressed

— "God doesn't love me."
— "I'm unforgivable."
— "I'm an abomination."
— "I'm an outcast."
— "No one will want me now."
— "I will be alone for the rest of my life."
— "God can never use me like this."

Statements parents of LGBTQ people might say when depressed

— "I don't know what to do."
— "We've lost a child."
— "I just don't know who my son or daughter is anymore."
— "My child's soul is going to be lost for all eternity."
— "What are other people going to think?"

How to move through depression

When depressed, we often think that the way we feel is going to last forever. These beliefs of irreversible despair are what move so many LGBTQ people to a place of hopelessness that becomes life-threatening. The most important thing to remember when you are feeling depressed is that this stage, just like every other, is normal and temporary. It will not last forever. Also remember that you are not alone. If you feel like you are in a dark place, reach out for help and support. Don't downplay your feelings or try to suppress your sadness. Instead, open yourself up to others and allow yourself to be seen and heard by a safe, trusted friend. People want to support you, but they can't if they don't know that you need them.

Acceptance

Acceptance is the stage when we come to terms with and begin to embrace the new normal set before us. We stop trying to push back against our LGBTQ identity, and we begin to embrace it and celebrate that which makes us unique in the world. It doesn't mean that everything is suddenly okay and we're now expected to be happy all the time, but rather that we've begun to be at peace with who we are and our load of grief is beginning to lighten.

Statements LGBTQ people might say or feel in acceptance

— "There are many other LGBTQ Christians who have come out before me. I'm not the only one."
— "God loves me and created me exactly the way I am."
— "I'm going to be okay."
— "It's going to get better."
— "I bring a unique diversity to the family of God that no one else can bring."
— "I can build a supportive community around me and create a family of choice."

Statements parents of LGBTQ people might say in acceptance

— "I don't understand, but I want to understand."
— "We value your honesty, even if it sometimes makes us uncomfortable."
— "If any of my friends or family have a problem with you, they have a problem with me too."
— "You deserve to be celebrated."
— "I love you"—without any "buts" or caveats.

How to live in acceptance

The more time that passes, the more fully you will begin to accept and embrace your (or your child's) LGBTQ identity. Take each day as it comes, allow yourself the grace to feel the emotions necessary for you to grieve and heal, surround your-self with people who will affirm you (and/or your LGBTQ loved one), and begin to claim that you are a beautiful child of God. Gradually, you will move more fully into this new reality and be able to love and celebrate the unique diversity of God that you get to display to the world.

SITTING WITH THE PROCESS OF GRIEF

Keep in mind that people often believe the myth that these stages of grief are a linear path, but in reality each stage can be experienced multiple times, or not at all. A stage may last weeks or only minutes before we bounce into another stage and then another. The important thing is to not put pressure on yourself to feel a certain way or heal before you're ready but to allow yourself the grace to float between stages of grief as they come. As you move back and forth through these stages of grief, know that the pain you feel is real, warranted, and valid.

The grief you are experiencing can be even more com-plicated if compounded by an additional unexpected loss, such as the death or illness of a loved one; a medical diag-nosis; a change in job, house, or location; or if you're going through a divorce. This is especially true for people in mixed-orientation marriages. If you were involved in ex-gay ther-apy, you were taught that your only option was to bridle your "same-sex attractions" and marry a person of the opposite gen-der. Following what leadership told you seemed right at the time, and in an effort to be pleasing to others and to God, you did as they instructed. But for many LGBTQ people, after marrying (and often having children and raising a family), they realize that they are unable to maintain this life over the long term. In order to be authentic, they not only have to come out, but many times they also end up dissolving their marriage in order to be fair to both partners' needs. As a result, the children have to grapple with the outcome. That is a lot of guilt and shame for any one person to carry around. Counseling with a licensed therapist is particularly important for people in this category. You need to know and understand in the depths of your soul that it is not your fault and never was.

Grappling with grief is also an opportunity to let go of your need to have all the answers and begin to live the questions. I came out in early 2012 and am far from having the answers to all my questions. In fact, I have more questions now than I did then. What has changed is my need to have all the answers. I've become comfortable with wonder, doubt, and uncertainty, which challenge me to learn and grow. Let it do the same for you. Begin to let go of your fear of the unknown and embrace it as an opportunity for growth. It will take you on a beautiful journey.

You can't hurry the grief process. You have to allow yourself to go through it and feel all of its deep and ugly emotions. But in the midst of that process, you should feel seen and heard and know that you belong in the family of God. So for the remainder of this chapter, let's explore some Bible passages that I hope will be a healing balm for your soul.

HEALING FOR THOSE WOUNDED BY CHURCH

As we've talked about in previous chapters, wounds from the church can be particularly painful because of the way it causes us to perceive God. We trust those in authority to teach us the Bible correctly, so when they tell us that being LGBTQ is a sin, we believe them; and when they teach a false doctrine, we regard it as truth.

One of the biggest drawbacks of the evangelical church is the lack of respect for critical thinking. Questioning a pastor's doctrine is seen as questioning God, which is considered blasphemous. Therefore, we don't dare to question anything at all. But that is not healthy. We need to think critically and not ever put anyone on too high of a pedestal. Everyone, regardless of their position or celebrity status, is human. We all have our own biases and lenses through which we see the world, and we all have the ability to hear God. Therefore, it would benefit us to listen to and learn from one another, rather than blindly accept what someone in authority says simply because they are deemed as one of God's elite. We are *all* God's elite, and nothing that you or anyone else does or says can change that.

When you are struggling to believe that you belong in the family of God, I encourage you to reflect on Romans 8:38–39 (NIV):

> For I am convinced that neither death nor life, neither angels nor demons, neither the present nor the future, nor any powers, neither height nor depth, nor anything else in all creation, will be able to separate us from the love of God that is in Christ Jesus our Lord.

Did you hear that? *Nothing* can separate you. Absolutely nothing. If I were to paraphrase this into a modern version of the text for today's LGBTQ people of God, it would say,

> For I am convinced that neither hate speech nor homophobic comments, neither rejection nor discrimination, neither depression nor anxiety, nor self-harm nor suicidal ideations, neither whom you love nor your gender identity, nor anything else that you fear or that others say about you in the name of God will ever be able to separate you from the love of God that is in Christ Jesus our Lord.

You belong, my friend. *You belong*, and absolutely *nothing* can ever change that. Rest in that and breathe it in deep into your soul. You bring a unique beauty to the family of God that no one else can offer, and you belong here, in it, with me and all the other beautiful LGBTQ Christians who add color to this far too often monochrome world.

When you struggle with how to treat those around you who are being hurtful or harming your soul because of how you identify or whom you love, meditate on this Scripture, which has always been one of my favorites:

Bless those who persecute you; bless and do not curse. Rejoice with those who rejoice, and weep with those who weep. Be of the same mind toward one another. Do not set your mind on high things, but associate with the humble. Do not be wise in your own opinion.

Repay no one evil for evil. Have regard for good things in the sight of all men. If it is possible, as much as depends on you, live peaceably with all men. . . . Therefore

"If your enemy is hungry, feed him;
"If he is thirsty, give him a drink;
"For in so doing you will heap coals of fire on his head."

Do not be overcome by evil, but overcome evil with good.
(Rom. 12:14–18, 20–21 NKJV)

By heaping coals of fire on their heads it doesn't mean throwing revenge or spite at those who have wronged you. Rather it means rising above, being the bigger person, keeping your heart clean, and leaving the rest up to God. I think our world would be much better off if we all strove to live by this passage of peace, authenticity, and wholeness. Don't you?

HEALING FOR THOSE REJECTED BY FAMILY

Nothing may be quite as painful as rejection by your family of origin for something you didn't choose and cannot change. Some days the notion seems so ridiculous to me that one person would banish another from their life simply because that person loves a man instead of a woman, or because their physical gender doesn't match who they know they are wired to be. I know reality is much more complicated and nuanced than that, but for those of you who share my story of rejection and loss of your biological family, and for those of you who still maintain contact even at the expense of it being uncomfortable and awkward, hear these words and let them soak your soul in healing waters.

When my father and my mother forsake me,
then the Lord will take care of me.
I would have lost heart, unless I had believed
That I would see the goodness of the Lord
In the land of the living.

Wait on the Lord;
Be of good courage,
And He shall strengthen your heart;
Wait, I say, on the Lord!
(Ps. 27:10, 13–14 NKJV)

Father to the fatherless, defender of widows—
this is God, whose dwelling is holy.
God places the lonely in families;
he sets the prisoners free and gives them joy.
(Ps. 68:5–6a)

Nothing has ever made me feel freer than deciding to be who I am and being unwilling to hide any longer. It has brought joy beyond anything I'd ever known before coming out. I want that for you too. I want you to feel the freedom that comes with being yourself, loving yourself, and embracing yourself—regardless of whether your family does or not. I want you to rest in the confidence that God smiles on you and will take care of you even if, and especially when, you feel like an orphan. When the psalmist says "God places the lonely in families," it doesn't mean all the pain vanishes. No one can replace the role of your biological family and be there in the way that your family should have been. However, surrogate family can help fill the gaps, and God amazingly brings them into our life exactly when we need them. Some people may only stay for a season; others may stay with you for life. I'm not going to tell you it suddenly becomes all sunshine and rainbows, because that is not the case. You may always have an empty space in your heart where your family should have been. But people will love and support you if you tap into the communities and resources around you. You are not alone. So

wait on the Lord, be of good courage, and let God strengthen
your heart.

HEALING FOR THOSE SCARRED
BY EX-GAY THERAPY

Ex-gay or reparative therapy is one of the most damaging
weapons to the LGBTQ soul still in existence. It is brainwash-
ing at its best and life-taking at its worst. It should never be
practiced on any human of any age and should be an illegal
practice worldwide. It is spiritual waterboarding. Reparative
therapists present their technique as possessing the capability to cure someone of "same-sex attraction" when, in reality,
they're merely instilling intense fear—fear of the wrath of God,
fear of death by AIDS, and fear of the need to have demons
exorcised from them—to the point that they are programmed
to abandon their "dangerous lifestyle" in order to not be sent to
hell for all eternity. It's abhorrent, and I am appalled that many
states still allow this practice.

That said, some LGBTQ people, myself included, suffer the
effects of ex-gay theology without ever having actually sat in an
official ex-gay therapy group. Why? Because this same theology is taught from pulpits, in youth groups, and in our homes.
As a result, we suffer many of the same repercussions as those
who actually attend ex-gay therapy: self-hatred, indoctrinated
beliefs that convince us we are horrible human beings whom
God can never use, fear that no one will ever want to be with
us because we are LGBTQ, and suicidal ideations, attempts,
and completions. Lives are being lost because of the atrocities
of conversion therapy. For any of you who have endured the
harm of ex-gay therapy to any degree, and for all of you who
have been tainted by its harmful theology, hear these words
from the psalmist David.

> Is anyone crying for help? GOD is listening,
> ready to rescue you.

If your heart is broken, you'll find GOD right there;
if you're kicked in the gut, he'll help you catch your
      breath.

Disciples so often get into trouble;
still, GOD is there every time.

He's your bodyguard, shielding every bone;
not even a finger gets broken.
(Ps. 34:17–20 MSG)

The LORD is close to the brokenhearted
  and saves those who are crushed in spirit.
(Ps. 34:18, NIV)

God sees your brokenness and the wrong done to you in the name of faulty religion. Jesus would surely not approve of this psychologically torturous act, nor would he ever interpret the Bible in that way. Jesus is close to you, he sees your wounds, and he will restore you more and more as you entrust your brokenness to God.

HEALING FOR THOSE WHO PERCEIVE REJECTION FROM GOD

If you've been told that you don't qualify for a place in the family of God because you are LGBTQ, it's hard to come away unscathed. Yes, we can heal from that and deconstruct our bad theology into a more accurate reflection of Jesus, but coming away without a lingering perception of God rejecting you is hard. But know this, my friends, and let it sink in to the very ground of your soul:

Therefore, there is now no condemnation for those who are in Christ Jesus, because through Christ Jesus the law of the Spirit who gives life has set you free from the law of sin and death.
(Rom. 8:1–2 NIV)

The Spirit gives life. The Spirit grants freedom to those who are in Christ Jesus, and *you* are *in* Christ Jesus. If you love Jesus, then Jesus is in you, and you are in him. Period. There's no caveat. And the law of sin and death is not that which damns you to hell for being LGBTQ; the law of sin and death is that which keeps you captive to the closet, keeps you hiding, and eats away at your soul. Freedom awaits you on the other side of living out your God-given LGBTQ identity. God embraces and celebrates the identity that was created in you from the very day you were born.

You have nothing to prove. You don't have to justify your existence to others. You don't have to prove to them that God loves you even though you are LGBTQ; you just have to know it. Believing it for yourself will ground you and give you the confidence you need so that you don't have to depend on other people's approval of you to be okay with who you are. What's more, you don't have to depend on their approval to know that God accepts you. You just know it because it sits at the very foundation of your soul. Stand firm and tall on that foundation. Be proud of who you are. The best is yet to come.

TO THE PARENT OR ALLY

This time of processing grief and loss is a critical period for your LGBTQ loved one. Be there for them. Ask them what they need. Maybe what they need is something really practical like someone to drive them to counseling. Maybe they just need a listening ear. Maybe they need to be included in your family so that they feel like they have a place to belong. Find out what they need most during this time and do your best to be that for them. Take time to give them a call or send them a text in the middle of the week to let them know you are thinking of them. When you've lost family and friends, your world can become eerily silent as people suddenly vanish from your life. Help fill that gap however you can. Ask your loved one how they are doing often and actually listen to the answer. It may be hard to hear sometimes, but they need someone to listen. Your presence in their life just might be the very thing that saves them, grants them hope, or gives them the will to live. It was for me.

A NOTE ON SUICIDE

If you are in a place of despair to the point that you are considering harming yourself or attempting suicide, or if you simply feel you are losing the will to live, *please* reach out to a trusted friend or adult who can help get you the support you need. Suicide is becoming an epidemic in our country, and you need to know that *your life has incredible value, and that you bring a beauty to the world that no one else can bring, simply by being yourself.* This transition is not easy, and it is not a road that anyone should try to travel alone. Allow the people you trust to come around you and support you during this critical time in your coming-out process. If you don't feel like you have anyone you can talk to, go to the list of free twenty-four-hour hotlines at the end of this book. Know that you can call, text, or chat with someone online at any time for support and a listening ear. Reach out to them. There is absolutely no shame in that. I've done it, as have many other LGBTQ people during times of loneliness or isolation. We all need someone to talk to, and we all feel less alone when we are heard by someone who cares.

10

Did You Not Know What the Divine Can Do with Your Diversity?

Embracing Who You Are

Your greatest self has been waiting your whole life; don't make it wait any longer.

—Steve Maraboli

"Did you not know what the Holy One can do with dust?" These words sat on the ground of my soul for an entire week following the Ash Wednesday service of 2017. I couldn't shake them or the power they held to resonate so deeply within me.

It had been five years since I'd attended an Ash Wednesday service. Because my dad grew up Catholic, we frequently observed Lent in our household when I was growing up, but as an adult, some years I've chosen to observe Lent and others I haven't. Some years, because of my conservative background, the pressure to conform to a custom simply for the sake of ritual (or, to me, what felt like measuring up) has been too cumbersome. Other years it has felt inviting—like an anchor that grounds me or gives me direction in life. Some years I have given something up for Lent, while other years I have added something to my life for that season.

But this was the first year my wife and I attended an Ash Wednesday service together. At first, I thought I was going more for her than for me. I had experienced this tradition before; she had not. But entering the silent sanctuary of our church that night, I realized I was wrong. I needed to be in this

151

space. Sitting in quiet reflection in a room lit only by candles, those small flames felt like beacons of hope in the dark. There was a peace present that my heart had been craving. I tried hard to slow my breathing and ground myself in the silence and calm provided.

In years past, before receiving the ashes, I've heard phrases like, "From dust you came, and to dust you will return," spoken as a solemn reminder of our humanity. But this year, I heard something different. This year, I heard words that were more than a depressing reminder of how mortal we are. These words came from a blessing by Jan Richardson called "Blessing the Dust," and as I listened, they became a breath of life that reminded me what God can do with us mere mortals.

One phrase in the blessing struck me unlike any other, and my eyes welled with tears. "Did you not know what the Holy One can do with dust?"[1] It was like God breathing and creating life out of the very dust and dirt on the ground of my soul just as was done with Adam in the creation story. Going forward to receive the ashes, a fellow congregant cupped my head in her hands, and repeated that exact phrase again while locking eyes with me.

"Did you not know what the Holy One can do with dust?"

It undid me. I couldn't contain my tears. So much of my life had felt marked by sorrow, shame, and loss. So many hopes had been tainted by the dust of life, by humanity, by mortality, by loss, by grief, or even by good intentions gone wrong. And yet . . . *and yet*, I had forgotten what God, the Holy One, can do with the dirt and dust of our lives. So often we underestimate the power of God to redeem and make beauty from the ashes. We forget that God is good and loves to meet us when we are at our lowest, and rescue and redeem and reclaim all that has been lost. As LGBTQ people, we also forget that the Divine can use not only the dust of our lives but also our diversity and uniqueness.

I love the song "This Is Me" from the movie *The Greatest Showman*. It is the perfect anthem for LGBTQ people. It encourages us to stand strong and look fear in the face, it honors our scars, and it declares that we are worthy of being celebrated exactly as we are. It's empowering. No matter how many times I listen to it, I get chills. My favorite version is the video of actress Keala Settle singing it for the first time with the band and other musicians.[2] Seeing her break free from her own insecurities in that epic moment was more than inspiring. It was magical.

Anytime someone overcomes adversity, it effects change for those who are watching. As Marianne Williamson says, "As we let our own light shine, we unconsciously give other people permission to do the same. As we are liberated from our own fear, our presence automatically liberates others."[3] We all have the ability to liberate others. When you confront who you are and decide to live unapologetically, you are freeing not only yourself but also others who are watching you: people you love, people who were against LGBTQ inclusion until it became someone they knew, people who are afraid to come out themselves, perhaps people who you don't even realize are watching. Your courage and bravery enlivens them to live boldly in their truth as well. It's like the butterfly effect—the idea that a small and seemingly insignificant event, like the fluttering of a butterfly's wings, can create tremendous and unexpected change in the world. So in the same vein as Jan Richardson, I would ask you, "Did you not know what the Divine can do with your diversity?" You have the power to embolden others simply by being yourself to the fullest. By loving and embracing who you are, and believing that God embraces you as well, you become a beacon of light to others who are struggling to confront their own fears. You can spark a flame inside them that propels them to live to their fullest potential, as you live out yours.

Perhaps the most inspiring element about "This Is Me" is that it is sung by a bunch of misfits—a group of people struggling to find their place of belonging in the world. Living to our fullest potential means embracing all that makes us human and whole—our height, our weight, our bodily features and shape, our physical limitations, our abilities or disabilities, our sexuality, our gender, our love, our skin color, our passions, and our dreams. It is saying, "Yes! This is who I am, and I am going to celebrate me and the diversity I bring to the world." We all have physical traits or characteristics that we view as flaws. We're so hard on ourselves that we never have to search very hard to find them. We spend so much of our lives trying to change who we are or how we look in order to fit into society's standards and cultural norms. Why do we fight so hard to be like everyone else? There is only one *you*—and you're it. You deserve to be seen and celebrated for who you are.

If I had to choose a favorite line in the song, which is hard for me because I think every line is beautiful and empowering, it would be in the bridge where Settle sings, "I know that I deserve your love, there is nothing that I'm not worthy of." Yes! *You deserve love! And being gay or lesbian or bisexual or transgender or gender-nonconforming or queer does not disqualify you from that. There is nothing that you are not worthy of!*

So chase after your dreams, my friends. Embrace the Divine diversity that God has placed within you. Walk confidently in who you are, and claim your place of belonging in the world. Be you to the very fullest, knowing that the God who created you loves you *exactly as you are.* You deserve to be seen. If you are willing to completely trust yourself and the God who made you and walk boldly into your calling, there is no telling what kind of change you might effect in the world. There is a life that you are destined to live, and only you can live it out.

Don't let anyone look down on you because of who you love. Rather, be an example to them of how to love well. Love deeply, love freely, love with all you have to give. God does not put restrictions on love. In fact, Jesus asks one thing of us and one thing only—that we love: that we love our neighbor (those around us), that we love ourselves (all of ourselves), and that we love God (who created us the way that we are). Regardless of what others may say, love, in all its diversity, makes the world a richer and more beautiful place. Love is meant to be seen and celebrated. You are worthy of love and belonging, my friends. So love freely, and live *unashamed.*

Acknowledgments

To my publisher, Westminster John Knox Press: Thank you for seeing the need for this book and for coming alongside me in working for LGBTQ equality within faith communities. Your work is pivotal in our fight for the dignity of all people.

To my editor, Jessica Miller Kelley: I'm so grateful that our vendor booths ended up next to one another at the QCF Conference in Denver. And I'm so thankful that you took the time to glance over to my table, abduct one of my books, and delve into it during your down time. Thank you for helping me see the need for this book and for convincing me it was not too soon to dive back into writing, and thank you for being such an incredible editor, cheerleader, and guide in this process. Your words of wisdom and expertise are coveted and valued. I'm honored to work with you.

To Elle Drumheller and the rest of the WJK marketing team: Thank you for your attention to detail, your expertise, and the effort you've put into making this book a success. I know your work often goes unnoticed, but no book can succeed without people like you working behind the scenes to make it happen. Thank you for your willingness to do an often thankless job.

To my wife, Clara: You are and always will be the love of my life. Thank you for believing in the work that I do, for grabbing takeout dinners on long writing days, for being willing to analyze a topic with me from all viewpoints, for whisking me away to the world of Heartland when my mind needs a break, and for being in the audience almost every time I speak. I couldn't do this without your support. I love you, cherish you, and am so lucky to call you mine.

To my honorary nana, Trish Young: I'll never be able to thank you enough for loving me like your own. You've truly become family to me, and that means more to me than mere words are able to express. I love you. Thank you for adopting both Clara and me into your heart.

To each of you who've shared your story with me during the creating of this book: Thank you for trusting me with your heart and allowing me to give your story a voice. I hope you feel that I've done it justice and honored your journey. Know that by sharing your story, others will feel less isolated in theirs.

To all the Mama Bears who reach out to me: I'm so grateful for your love, encouragement, and support. You give me hope and lend me strength when the days of working for equality wear me down. Keep spreading a message of love to your LGBTQ kids and to those who need a Mama Bear in their life. I know I still do.

To my readers and followers: Thank you for your encouragement, for putting up with my sporadic blogging, and for believing in the work that I do. Thank you for reading, following, and sharing my work. And thank you to each of you who have taken time to write me and share your personal stories. I read every one of them. This book is for you. You are the reason I write and the inspiration that gets me out of bed to work for equality each day.

Finally, I am thankful for the love of God that captivates me, the wonder of God that holds me in awe, and the diversity of God that constantly reminds me just how beautiful this family of God really is.

Notes

Chapter 1: You Are Not Broken

1. Erin O. White, *Given Up for You* (Madison: University of Wisconsin Press, 2018).

2. "Preventing Suicide: Facts about Suicide," The Trevor Project, www.thetrevorproject.org.

3. Christopher Ingraham, "More Than 26,000 Children and Teens Have Been Killed in Gun Violence since 1999," *Washington Post*, March 23, 2018.

4. Brené Brown, "Listening to Shame," TED Talk, youtube.com.

Chapter 2: Claiming Hope

1. Marianne Williamson, *A Return to Love: Reflections on the Principles of* A Course in Miracles (New York: HarperCollins, 1992), 190–91.

Chapter 3: We Need One Another

1. Mark Tidd, Highlands Church Denver, used with permission.

Chapter 7: Am I Worth It?

1. Nadia Bolz-Weber, "Why You Should Forgive Assholes," www.facebook.com/makerswomen/videos/1546052612169724/UzpfSTE
wMDAwMDY3OTc5MTY3NDoxOTQ0NzU1NzgyMjIzNzI5/.

Chapter 9: If Your Heart Is Aching

1. Richard Rohr, "Emotional Sobriety: Rewiring Our Programs for Happiness," Center for Contemplation and Action, https://cac.org.

2. Some of the resources aiding in this adaptation of Kübler-Ross's five stages of grief are: "The Five Stages of Grief," grief.com; "Five Stages of Grief" chart, https://journeytogenius.files.wordpress.com/2011/02/5grief_stages630x821.png; and John B. Mahaffie, "Stages of Grief" table, available at https://foresightculture.com/wp-content/uploads/Foresight-stages-of-grief-3.jpg.

Chapter 10: Did You Not Know What the Divine Can Do with Your Diversity?

1. Jan Richardson, "Blessing the Dust," in *Circle of Grace: A Book of Blessings for the Seasons* (Orlando, FL: Wanton Gospeller Press, 2015), 89.

2. "This Is Me," with Keala Settle, from *The Greatest Showman* (dir. Michael Gracey), www.youtube.com.

3, Marianne Williamson, *A Return to Love: Reflections on the Principles of* A Course in Miracles (New York: HarperCollins, 1992), 191.

Recommended Resources

For Further Reading

Beeching, Vicky. *Undivided*. New York: HarperOne, 2018.

Brown, Brené. *Braving the Wilderness*. New York: Random House, 2017.

Brown, Brené. *The Gifts of Imperfection*. Minneapolis: Hazelden Publishing, 2010.

Cantorna, Amber. *Refocusing My Family*. Minneapolis: Fortress Press, 2017.

Gushee, David. *Changing Our Mind*. Third edition. Canton, MI: Read the Spirit Books, 2017.

Hartke, Austen. *Transforming*. Louisville, KY: Westminster John Knox Press, 2018.

Martin, Colby. *Unclobber*. Louisville, KY: Westminster John Knox Press, 2016.

Pasquale, Teresa B. *Sacred Wounds*. St. Louis: Chalice Press, 2015.

White, Erin O. *Given Up for You*. Madison: University of Wisconsin Press, 2018.

Organizations

The Christian Closet (thechristiancloset.com): An online therapeutic resource for people who are trying to work out what it means to have an LGBTQ sexual identity within a Christian context.

Church Clarity (churchclarity.org): An organization creating a new standard for how churches communicate their actively enforced policies on LGBTQ inclusion.

FreedHearts (freedhearts.org): A faith-based organization for parents of LGBTQI children that frees hearts to love, heal, and affirm.

Q Christian Fellowship (qchristian.org): A Christian ministry offering both online and offline support to LGBTQ Christians and allies by creating safe spaces to make friends, ask questions, and receive and offer help.

The Reformation Project (reformationproject.org): An organization training Christians to support and affirm lesbian, gay, bisexual, and transgender people.

Hotlines

National Hopeline Network
www.hopeline.com
1.800.SUICIDE (784.2433)

National Suicide Prevention Lifeline
www.suicidepreventionlifeline.org
1.800.273.TALK (8255)

The Trevor Project
www.thetrevorproject.com
1.866.488.7386

For a more extensive list of
available resources, please visit
AmberCantorna.com.

CPSIA information can be obtained
at www.ICGtesting.com
Printed in the USA
FFHW010256020319
50772530-56190FF